ImproperBostonians

Lesbian and gay history
from the Puritans
to Playland

Improper Bostonians

Compiled by
The History Project

Foreword by
Barney Frank

Beacon Press   Boston

Beacon Press
25 Beacon Street
Boston, Massachusetts

Beacon Press books are published under the auspices of
the Unitarian Universalist Asssociation of Congregations.

04 03 02 01 00 99   8 7 6 5 4 3 2

Text design by John Kane

Library of Congress Cataloging-in-Publication Data
Improper Bostonians : lesbian and gay history from the Puritans
    to Playland / compiled by the History Project ; foreword by Barney Frank.
            p.   cm.
        ISBN 0-8070-7948-0 (cloth)
        ISBN 0-8070-7949-9 (paper)
        1. Lesbians—Massachusetts—Boston—History. 2. Gay men—
        Massachusetts—Boston—History. I. History Project (Boston, Mass.)
    HQ76.3.U52M45 1998
    305.9'0664'0974461—dc 21   98–11928

THIS ORGANIZATION IS FUNDED IN PART BY

MASSACHUSETTS CULTURAL COUNCIL
A state agency that supports public programs in the arts, humanities, and sciences

To the generations before us, for what they endured
To the generations to come, and better times

Table of contents

Acknowledgments

For The History Project:

Curators
Libby Bouvier
Kim Markert
Stephen Nonack
Nancy Richard
Editor
Neal Kane
Designer
John Kane

This book draws heavily from research conducted since 1980 by The History Project (originally known as the Boston Area Lesbian and Gay History Project). We offer our thanks to all those who have participated in the organization over the years; to the distinguished historians and writers whose published and unpublished research we consulted in the preparation of *Improper Bostonians;* and to the institutions that kindly permitted use of materials from their collections.

The History Project is a nonprofit organization supported by hundreds of individuals who have donated their time, money, and services to our efforts. We thank you all. We are also grateful for the support of our many sponsors, notably the Massachusetts Cultural Council, a state agency; the Boston Cultural Council, a municipal agency supported by the Massachusetts Cultural Council; Boston Lesbian and Gay Communities Funding Partnership: A Special Initiative of the Boston Foundation and Collaborating Funding Partners; and the Scott Opler Foundation, Inc. Warmest thanks to Arthur Dion and Virginia Anderson at Gallery NAGA for their ongoing support.

In particular, we thank Les Brewer, whose boundless generosity made this book possible, and the staff at Unison (formerly Boris Image Group).

We thank our friends at Beacon Press for their vision, advice, and enthusiasm throughout this project—particularly Helene Atwan, Deb Chasman, Sara Eisenman, Dan Ochsner, and Susan Worst. Thanks also to our copy editor Katie Blatt.

Finally, we wish to thank the individuals, past and present, whose voices spoke to us across the years, and now will continue to speak.

The following historians, writers, and individuals were consulted in conjunction with the preparation of *Improper Bostonians* (where requested, we have only used an individual's last initial):

Joy B.
Jimmy Boynton
Kathleen Bragdon
Michael Bronski
Adrian Cathcart
Preston Claridge
Bill Conrad
Deb Edel
Alice Foley
Mr. G.
Robert G.
Richard Godbeer
Andrew L. Gray
Barbara Hoffman
Catherine Kaplan
Kate Clifford Larson
Mark J. Laughlin
Jim McGrath
Paul McMahon
Janet Miller
Frank Morgan
Steve Nichols
Robert Reed
Marilyn Richardson
Conrad S.
Jean S.
Douglass Shand-Tucci
Richard Shibley
Sylvia Sidney
Chester Solomon
Francis Toohey
Lisa Tuite
Susan von Salis
Susan Wilson
Louise Y.
Donald Yacovone
Helaine Zimmerman

A number of institutions, particularly the Boston Athenæum, were extremely generous in providing source material from their rich collections:

American Antiquarian Society
Andover Newton Theological School
Boston Athenæum
Boston Globe Library
Boston Public Library Fine Arts, Microtext, Print, Rare Books and Manuscripts, and Social Sciences Departments
Brookline Public Library
College of the Holy Cross
Haffenreffer Museum
Harvard Law School Library, Manuscript Unit
Harvard Theater Collection
Harvard University Archives
Houghton Library
Maine Archaeological Society
Massachusetts Historical Society
Massachusetts Supreme Judicial Court Archives
Moorland-Spingarn Research Center
New Bedford Whaling Museum
New York Public Library, Rare Books and Manuscripts Division
Norwood Historical Society
Old North Church, Marblehead
Schlesinger Library, Radcliffe College
Society for the Preservation of New England Antiquities
Sturgis Library, Barnstable
Tozzer Library, Harvard University
Wellesley College Archives

Foreword

In a better world, the line between the political and the personal would be more easily discerned. This means, paradoxically, that activities which impinge on the privacy of the departed contribute to the fight for the privacy rights of lesbian and gay inhabitants of the present and the future.

Improper Bostonians illustrates that paradox. It draws on intimate facts about those who have preceded us—sometimes in ways that would have disturbed them—in order better to defend the rights of contemporary gay people to live our lives free of the incursions of homophobic prejudice.

That this movement has recently met with a considerable degree of success is one of the facts which this volume demonstrates. Incidents of private parties broken up by the police, and of individuals jailed merely for kissing someone of the same sex—or dressing like someone of the other—fortunately seem extremely remote to those of us who live in Boston today. Yet some of these horror stories date back no more than thirty years.

That the same movement still has a considerable distance to go is, unfortunately, an equally relevant fact—as will be demonstrated by critics of this volume, who will object to the decision to reveal what they consider to be unseemly data about respected figures who, they argue, should be allowed to rest undisturbed by speculation—or even worse, proof—of their homosexuality.

This is precisely why the sort of history presented here is welcomed by those of us who do not believe that these facts ought to be considered unseemly. It is our experience that homophobia is a prime example of the truth that prejudice survives on ignorance, and is best defeated by knowledge.

Indeed, our recognition of the value of historical volumes in defeating prejudice is informed by our experience that nothing has been of greater value in the fight for fair treatment of gay men and lesbians than the contemporary phenomenon known as "coming out"—the act of being honest about one's sexual orientation.

"Being honest" is the operative phrase here. People who complain that they are being told more than they want to know about the private lives of lesbians, gay men, and bisexuals are, often without realizing it, not only objecting to honesty, but arguing in favor of outright deception. Historically, it is reasonable to argue that the fact of someone's homosexuality should be ignored by his or her biographers only if one is prepared to argue that no other basic facts of the private lives of prominent people should be recounted.

Contemporaneously, those who assert that, while they have no objection to someone else's homosexuality, they do not see why the gay man or lesbian in question has to make that fact known, ignore a fundamental fact about everyday life: it is impossible to go forty-eight hours in society and answer the casual conversational questions of friends and relatives without either revealing one's sexual orientation or lying about it.

This book rests on the premise that discussions of people's sexual orientation should not be exempt from the notion that honesty is the best policy, and that those who argue for deception carry a heavy burden of proof which they cannot meet.

Barney Frank
Representative, U.S. 4th District, Massachusetts

Introduction

The History Project is a volunteer group of archivists, historians, researchers, writers, designers, and activists committed to uncovering, preserving, and presenting the rich contributions of lesbians and gay men over three and a half centuries of Boston history. In June 1996, we presented our work to date in an exhibit—**Public Faces/Private Lives: Boston's Lesbian and Gay History**—at the Boston Public Library, where it was viewed by over 55,000 people. The exhibit subsequently traveled to Salem State College in October 1996 and the Boston Center for the Arts in June 1997. At each location, dozens of people asked us the same question: "Why isn't this a book?" Now it is.

Public Faces/Private Lives: Boston's Lesbian and Gay History—exhibit installation at the Boston Public Library, June 1996. The exhibit was the best attended in the library's history.

The reason for such an undertaking is simple, and is perhaps best explained by a simple example. Millions of people travel annually to Rome to view Michelangelo's ceiling in the Sistine Chapel—one of the great achievements in Western culture. They accept as an historical fact that he was an Italian living in the sixteenth century; for Italians, his accomplishment is a source of national pride.

Less well known, and less accepted, is the fact that he was a homosexual. The latter fact, like the former, does not intrinsically amplify or diminish the work itself. For gay people everywhere, however, his sexuality engenders a similar sense of pride. It says to us something akin to what it says to Italians: We are here. We have always been here. One of us did this. We matter.

Unlike most other self-identified groups, gay people have grown up without realistic images of those like us who came before. We, and the world around us, came of age without any sense that gay people existed, let alone that they were vibrant participants in their communities and their culture. Imagine the connection an isolated gay teenager might experience while looking at a John Singer Sargent painting, knowing that the artist was gay. Or the inspiration a young lesbian might feel while singing "America the Beautiful," knowing that its lyricist, Katharine Lee Bates, lived happily with her partner, Katharine Coman, for twenty-five years. It is for the people growing up now, and the people who are raising them, that we have assembled this book.

In three important ways, we were lucky to be living in Boston when we undertook this project. Founded in 1630, Boston has a history virtually as old as the history of Europeans in America; documenting homosexuality here means documenting it back to our nation's origins. For the next two and a half centuries, Boston's mores occupied a central place in the nation's zeitgeist; lesbians and gay men living here significantly influenced the thoughts and aspirations of all Americans. In the last century, the struggle of working gay men and lesbians in Boston to make a place for themselves in society accurately mirrors the struggle of gay people across the country. Boston's story is everyone's story.

Because our method has been to work with source material (and Boston's archives are rich), our aim is to present documents, photographs, letters, and reminiscences with only enough commentary to provide a context for their inclusion. Happily, scores of historians are currently producing the significant works required to afford gay people their rightful place in History. At the same time, we feel that the material compiled for this book speaks eloquently for itself. One of the great joys to date in presenting our exhibit has been to overhear any number of people—old, young, gay, and straight—saying to themselves, "I didn't know that."

The terms *lesbian* and *gay* are modern in origin. The invention of homosexuality itself is as recent as the beginning of the twentieth century. In researching the lives of people who might today identify themselves as lesbians or gay men, we looked for those individuals in the past who led unconventional lives, who flouted the established rules, who were unapologetic about the styles of life they adopted, and who preferred the company of members of their own sex. In many cases, our attraction to these extraordinary people was intuitive. We do not assume that all of them are gay; at the same time, knowing what we know about them and about ourselves, we cannot assume that all of them were straight.

As with most underdocumented groups in our society, lesbian and gay history does not easily reveal itself. Libraries and archives have only just begun to reexamine their collections for social and cultural information about the lives of people of color, the poor, women, children, immigrants, sexual minorities, and others who were not wealthy white men. The process of recataloging and reindexing has far to go, and we hope that this book encourages that work.

While we took pains to represent people of color and those from diverse economic and social classes, we found that most letters and diaries kept and preserved before 1900 were by those from advantaged groups; privileged men and women were most likely to have written about themselves or to have had information published about them. To a lesser extent, this is also true for the period leading up to the Stonewall riots. The lack of comprehensive documentation presents a crit-

ical problem in the formation of a truly balanced history of lesbian and gay Boston. It also demonstrates the need for permanent lesbian and gay archives, repositories for the evidence that reveals how we all live, work, love, and die.

In preparing this book, we have discovered men and women who struggled to lead whole lives and who fought to express themselves as active, creative, loving, and, yes, sexual human beings. It is with pleasure that we tell their stories.

4 "I find my spirit so exceedingly carried with love to my pupils that I can't tell how to take up my rest in God."

From the diary of Michael Wigglesworth (5 April 1653)

A page from Michael Wigglesworth's journal, showing entries in the code he used to record his "unclean" thoughts

A Puritan heritage: The seventeenth century

From the founding of Plymouth Colony and Massachusetts Bay Colony, the mission of Boston Puritan leadership was the creation of a Christian commonwealth based on biblical teachings and strict gender and social hierarchies: God/man, man/woman, father/son. The Puritan family—"the little commonwealth"—was a reflection of that need for order. In 1677, the church in Dorchester charged its members "to Reforme our famelys…. Restraining them as much as in us lyeth, from all evil and especially the Sins of the times." A common ideal for the period, "family government" was a model of obedience to a male patriarch, modified only by a wife's contributions as mistress of domestic duties. The Puritan "household" was, for the most part, similar to a modern nuclear family, but often included servants, boarders, widows, and orphans. Both the colonies of Massachusetts Bay and Plymouth enacted laws requiring unwed single persons to live within an established household, ensuring scrupulous monitoring of "disorderly living" and sexual deviance. Since the purpose of marriage was to follow biblical commands to replenish the earth, sexual relations that were not procreative and that were outside the ordinance of marriage were considered threatening. These included fornication, adultery, masturbation, and especially bestiality and sodomy.[1]

For the Puritans, sodomy occupied a place in the imagination that is almost unintelligible to modern understanding. In his 1674 sermon "The Cry of Sodom," the Reverend Samuel Danforth of Duxbury drew an explicit parallel between the biblical city of Sodom and the settlements of New England. According to Danforth, allowing sodomitical behavior to go unpunished was to risk calling down the wrath of God upon the state, just as the sins of Sodom and Gomorrah provoked fire from the Heavens. Because of its consequences for the entire community, sodomy was considered a political crime as much as a physical act, in which the order of the world and its gender relationships were turned upside down.[2]

Regardless of the symbolic meanings of sodomy for the early Puritans, the statistics for discovery and prosecution are few for this capital offense. Historians have suggested that the Puritans were reluctant to accuse members of their communities of craving "strange flesh." Only two executions in New England were reported for the act of sodomy. Obtaining evidence for sodomy was difficult, since two witnesses were required for conviction. Much more frequently, court documents record "lewd" activities (ones that we would now call homosexual) that were not punished with death. The Reverend John Raynor of Plymouth spoke of the difficulty of discovering sodomitical acts, since, unlike fornication or adultery, there was no possibility of pregnancy.[3]

By the second and third generations after the Great Migration of the Puritans to New England, signs of social and intellectual stress appeared—King Philip's War, rival religious sects, witch trials, the loss of colonial self-government. As a result of these developments, the Puritan clergy began to lose its exclusive control over the religious life of the colony and over the power of the state to regulate sexual behavior.[4]

Native Americans and homosexuality

The sexual culture of the Indians of North America was profoundly different from that of the Europeans, and became one of the principal justifications for their enslavement and conquest. By the 1980s, historians had documented more than one hundred thirty North American tribes with positive social roles for both gay men and lesbian women. Sometimes called *berdache,* cross-dressing male homosexuals made important contributions to Indian religion, medicine, war making, and child rearing. European settlers also observed the participation of "women warriors" in a variety of tribal contexts.[5]

Seventeenth-century European observers of New England Native American life, such as Roger Williams, Thomas Morton, and Edward Winslow, recorded examples of the Indians' attitudes toward sexuality. Among the southeastern New England Indians, premarital relations were permissible and obtaining divorces was relatively simple. Beyond that, little has been documented.

Although the evidence for tribal groups in other areas of the continent is extensive, additional research is needed to enlarge our understanding of the sexual practices and attitudes of the New England Indian tribes before the Europeans. To date, this has been impeded by a number of factors. Many of the tribal villages of New England were depopulated by disease before the arrival of the English, and settlers found vast areas of uninhabited land. By the time of King Philip's War in 1675, armed skirmishes, slavery, and the herding of Christianized Indians into "Praying Towns" had furthered the early destruction of New England Indian culture and society.[6]

Erotic Native American
petroglyphs found along
the Kennebec River,
Solon, Maine

Capitall Laws

94

Deut 13·6·10
Deut. 17·2·6
Ex. 22·20

If any man after legall conviction shall haue or worship
any other god, but ye lord god, he shall be put to death.

2

Ex. 22·18.
Lev. 20·27.
Deut. 18·10·

If any man or woeman be a witch, (that is hath or con=
sulteth with a familiar spirit, they shall be put to death.

3

Lev. 24·15·16

If any person shall blaspheme ye name of god, the father, —
sonne or Holie ghost, with direct, expresse, presumptuous
or high handed blasphemie, or shall curse god in ye like —
manner, he shall be put to death.

4

Ex. 21·12·
Numb. 35·13
14·30·31·

If any person comitt any wilfull murther, which is man -
slaughter, comitted vpon premeditated mallice hatred,
or crueltie, not in a mans necessarie & iust defence,
nor by meere casualtie against his will. he shall be
put to death.

5

Num. 25·20
21·
Lev. 24·17.

If any person slayeth an other suddainely in his anger
or crueltie of passion, he shall be put to death.

6

Ex. 21·14.

If any person shall slay an other through guile, either by
poysoning or other such divelish practise, he shall be put to death.

7

Lev. 20·15·
16.

If any man or woeman shall lye with any beast or bruite
creature by Carnall Copulation, they shall surely be put to
death. And ye beast shall be slaine, & buried & not eaton

8

Lev. 20·13.

If any man lyeth with man kinde as he lyeth with a woeman, both
of them haue comitted abhomination, they both shall surely
be put to death.

9

Lev. 20·19·
18·20·
Deut. 22·24·
24·

If any person comitteth Adultery with a maried or espoused wife
the Adulterer & Adulteresse shall surely be put to death.

10

Ex. 21·16·

If any man stealeth a man or man kinde, he shall surely be put
to death.

11

Deut. 19·16·
18·19·

If any man rise vp by false witnes, wittingly & of purpose
to take away any mans life; he shall be put to death.

12

If any man shall conspire & attempt any invasion, insurrec=
tion, or publique rebellion agt ye comon wealth. or shall in=
deavour to surprise any towne or townes, fort or forts therein,
or shall treacherously & perfidiouslie attempt ye alteration
& subversion of our frame of politie or gouernment funda=
mentallie, he shall be put to death.   A declaration

S·1

S·2

S·3

S·4

S·5

S·6

S·7

S·8

S·9

S·10

S·11

S·12

Massachusetts Bay *Body of Liberties*, 1641. Article 8 prohibits sodomy.

Sodomy and the law

Dozens of antisodomy statutes were passed in New England during the seventeenth century. The earliest statutes combined the language of existing British laws, such as King Henry VIII's 1533 Buggery Act, with biblical proscriptions against same-sex behavior. Later statutes eliminate biblical references and make appeals to "natural" law.[7]

1636
"Sodomy, rapes, buggery" are among eight offenses punishable by death at New Plymouth Colony.

1641
Massachusetts Bay passes a sodomy law in its *Body of Liberties:*

If any man lyeth with man kinde as he lyeth with a woman, both of them have comitted abhomination, they both shall surely be put to death.

1642
The General Court of Connecticut lists sodomy as a capital crime.

1647
Rhode Island includes sodomy in a category of capital crimes called "touching Whoremongers."

1656
New Haven Colony enacts an inclusive capital law against same-sex relations: men lying with men, acts of women "against nature," and masturbation in the sight of others.

1680
New Hampshire's sodomy law states, "They shall both surely be put to death."[8]

The love of David and Jonathan

A number of historians have pointed to growing confusion in the early seventeenth century over the meaning of "masculine" friendships. Custom allowed men to express love for one another openly—even to become "bedfellows"—without the accusation of sodomy. Questions were rarely raised unless such relationships subverted the social order through favoritism toward a servant or through undue influence over a social superior. James I of England, in his 1617 Privy Council, felt such a need to defend himself against charges of sodomy toward his favorite, George Villiers, the earl of Buckingham: "You may be sure that I love the Earl of Buckingham more than anyone else, and more than you who are here assembled. I wish to speak in my own behalf and not to have it thought to be a defect, for Jesus Christ did the same, and therefore I cannot be blamed. Christ had his son John, I have my George."[9]

Perhaps one of the best examples of this ambivalence over same-sex love comes from John Winthrop, first governor of the Massachusetts Bay Colony. On the one hand, he felt comfortable declaring his love for Sir William Springe prior to his sailing to North America. Later, however, Winthrop supported the execution for sodomy of William Plaine of Guilford when approached by the leadership of New Haven Colony.

Letter from John Winthrop to William Springe, 8 February 1630:

I loved you truly before I could think that you took any notice of me: but now I embrace you and rest in your love: and delight to solace my first thoughts in these sweet affections of so dear a friend. The apprehension of your love and worth together hath overcome my heart, and removed the veil of modesty, that I must needs tell you, my soul is knit to you, as the soul of Jonathan to David: were I now with you, I should bedew that sweet bosom with the tears of affection....

O what a pinch will it be to me, to part with such a friend! if any Emblem may express our Condition in heaven, it is this Communion in love.[10]

This excerpt from John Winthrop's *History of New England* describes the execution of William Plaine in 1646:

Plaine of Guilford being discovered to have used some unclean practices, upon examination and testimony, it was found, that being a married man, he had committed sodomy with two persons in England, that he had corrupted a great part of the youth of Guilford by masturbations, which he had committed, and provoked others to the like above a hundred times; and to some who questioned the lawfulness of such filthy practice, he did insinuate seeds of atheism, questioning whether there was a God, etc. The magistrates and elders (so many as were at hand) did all agree, that he ought to die, and gave divers reasons from the word of God. And indeed it was *horrendum facinus* [a dreadful crime], and he a monster in human shape, exceeding all human rules and examples that ever had been heard of, and it tended to the frustrating of the ordinance of marriage and the hindering of the generation of mankind.[11]

John Winthrop

14

An early-twentieth-
century representation of
the maypole at
Merrymount

The seal of Quincy,
Massachusetts, showing
Merrymount

In the late 1620s, Thomas Morton founded his own colony on a site he dubbed "Merrymount" at Wollaston in present-day Quincy. He sometimes called his colony "Mary-mount" or "Mare-mount," playing on connotations of sodomy, buggery, and, possibly, Catholicism, in order to shock the Puritans. To the displeasure of the authorities, Morton revived the "pagan" practice of maypole dancing in 1637, and set himself up as the "Lord of Misrule," a comic Renaissance master of ceremonies. According to William Bradford, Morton also established a "School of Atheism," which was a word employed by other writers of the period to imply sodomy. Bradford wrote in 1642:

Marvelous it may be to see and consider how some kind of wickedness did grow and break forth here.... But that which is worse, even sodomy and buggery (things fearful to name) have broke forth in this land oftener than once.[12]

Bradford on Morton's Merrymount:

They also set up a maypole, drinking and dancing about it many days together, inviting the Indian women for their consorts, dancing and frisking together like so many fairies, or furies, rather; and worse practices.

In the first passage, Bradford makes the "worse practices" of sodomy and buggery explicit; in the second, the worse practices are implied. His description of Merrymount also evokes the specter of interracial sexual relations, thus emphasizing Morton's outlaw sexuality.[13]

By publishing *New English Canaan* in 1637, Morton became one of the few early European observers to find dignity and worth in the landscape and native peoples of the New World. In contrast to the Puritans, Morton did not see the New World as a desert wilderness but as a land rich in erotic fulfillment and natural abundance.

In his account of the maypole of Merrymount, Morton mocks the Pilgrim leaders, calling Miles Standish and John Endicott "Captain Shrimp" and "Captain Littleworth," respectively. In those passages, Morton reinforces the image of "disordered" sexuality by dedicating a poem to Oedipus and other heroes with unusual sexual proclivities. He also refers to "Ganymede and Jupiter," a Renaissance code phrase for homosexual relations.

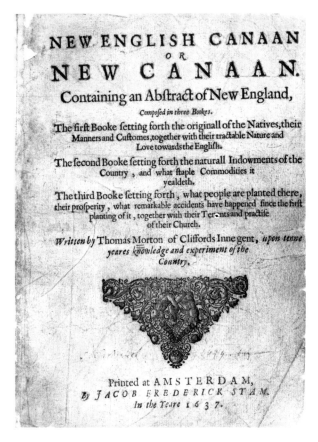

Whatever the Puritans thought of his sexual activities, Morton's fraternization with the Indians proved to be too much for the colonial authorities. He was accused of selling weapons to the "savages" and extradited to England. When Morton returned to New England, the Puritans imprisoned him for a year in Boston without adequate heat, food, or clothing. He died soon after his release.[14]

> And be it further enacted by the Authority aforesaid that if any ☻man shall wear ☻Mens Aparell; or if any ☻man shall wear ☻mens Aparrel, and be thereof duely convicted, they shall be Corporally punished or fined, at the discretion of the Quarter Sessions, not exceeding five pounds, to the use of the County where the offence is comitted to be towards the defreying of the County charges.

> Deborah Byar convict by Testimonies & by her owne confession of putting on men's Apparrell at severall times & places, once in a publick house. The Court Order her to stand one houre on a stoole near the Cage in Boston on a Lecture Day after Lecture with a Paper on her Breast. FOR putting on mans apparell and to give bond for her good behaviol in ten pounds with Sureties till the next Court of this County paying fees of Court. &c
> John Hill & Henry Ingraham both of Boston entred into Recognizance of ten pou: before the Court.

Top:
The original 1695 draft of a Massachusetts law, recently uncovered in the Massachusetts Archives, enacted against wearing clothing of the opposite sex. The law imposed a penalty of five pounds or corporal punishment.

Bottom:
In 1691, the Suffolk County Court sentenced Deborah Byar to submit a ten-pound bond, and to stand on a stool in a public place with a paper on her breast that read: "For putting on man's apparel."

Puritans in drag

Cross-dressing was a small component in the homosexual "Molly" subculture of late-seventeenth-century London, but no evidence exists for colonial transgendered activity as an expression of group identity. (*Molly* was a word used to describe an effeminate man or boy.) In fact, no court case from the seventeenth century links cross-dressing to homosexuality. The public violation of gender roles through cross-dressing would have been the actual threat to the orderly patriarchy of Puritan society, not homosexuality.

The Reverend Nicholas Noyes (1647-1717), a longtime Salem pastor and leader in the persecution of witches, published *An Essay Against Periwigs* (1672) in which he described the wearing of wigs by men as the removal of "one notable, visible distinction of sex." He compared it to cross-dressing, citing Deuteronomy 22:5: "The woman shall not wear that which pertaineth unto a man, neither shall a man put on a woman's garment: for all that do so are abomination unto the LORD thy God." Wigs, according to Noyes, were "a kind of monstrosity" that presented "an unnatural incongruity between the complexion and hair, when the complexion and constitution is masculine and the hair feminine."[15]

This 1677 court record describes a woman who was brought to court for dressing as a man:

Dorothie Hoyt, called into court upon her presentment for putting on man's apparel, made default, she having gone out of the county. Her father, John Hoyt, appeared and owned the fact, manifesting Dorothie's repentance, and desiring to fall under the penal part of the sentence. It was ordered that she be apprehended as soon as she returned, and be severely whipped unless her father forthwith pay a fine of 40s. in corn or money.[16]

The following 1652 case from New Hampshire emphasizes the disorderly and public scandal of a cross-dressing violation:

Whereas at the Courte holden at Salisbury the 13 of the month ([16]52) Josepth Davis of Haverill beinge presented for puttinge on woemans apparell and goeinge aboute from house to house in the nighte and Mary Peaslye accompaninge him, which mary peasly was also prsented for going with the saide Joseph Davis in the nighte, and for as much as the saide Josepthe davis & mary peasly beinge removed from haverill into this Jurisdiction and beinge apprehended and broughte into the foresaide

Courte heare holden at strawberey banke the 9 of the 8 month (52) [that] is ordered by the Courte that Joseph Davis is Judged to paye [a ten-shilling] fine, and also to make publike acknowledgment of his fault on a cer-taine daye at haverell before the next Courte.[17]

Because relations between women did not fit the strictly penetrative model of sodomy, Puritan lawmakers rarely leg-islated against women. They were much more threatened by the possi-blity of unions between male animals and women. Only New Haven Colony formally included women in its lists of sex crimes. New Haven lawmakers quoted St. Paul: "And: if any woman change the natural use, into that which is against nature as Rom. 1:26 she shall be liable to the same sentence, and punishment [of death]."[18]

The following court account was origi-nally bowdlerized by an early twentieth-century editor. The clause in italic was not transcribed:

Elizabeth Johnson, servant to Mr. Jos. yonge, to be severly whipped and fined 5 [shillings] for unseemly prac-tices betwixt her and another maid *attempting to do that which man and woman do;* also for stubbornness to her mistress answering rudely and unman-nerly; and also for stopping her ears with her hands when the Word of God was read.[19]

In 1649, Sarah Norman (who was later involved with a group of men brought to court for homosexual behavior) and Mary Hammon appeared before the New Plymouth Colony Court:

Wheras the wife of Hugh Norman, of Yarmouth, hath stood presented divers Courts for misdemenior and lude behavior with Mary Hammon uppon a bed, with divers lasivious speeches by her allso spoken, but shee could not apeere by reason of som hinder-ances until this court, the said Court have therefore sentanced her, the said wife of Hugh Norman, for her vile behavior in the aforsaid particulars, to make a publick acknowlidgment, so fare as conveniently may bee, of her unchast behavior, and have allso warned her to take heed of such cariages for the future, lest her former cariage come in remembrance against her to make her punishment the greater.[20]

Reconstructing the gay and lesbian experience before the late twentieth century requires creative examination of sporadic information often drawn from court records: homosexual acts were capital crimes until the early nineteenth century. Information on homosexual life in seventeenth-century New England is sketchy, and there is no evidence for claiming the existence of a gay subculture. However, the aforementioned court records suggest that men and women with same-sex attractions found others like themselves and formed long-term relationships and networks. Searching through cases in the records for Plymouth, historian Robert Oaks speculates about the relationship of Richard Berry and Teage Joanes.

Most suggestive is the case of Richard Berry and Teage Joanes. In 1649, Berry accused Joanes of sodomy, and both were ordered to attend the next court for trial. Berry also claimed that Joanes committed "unclean practisses" with Sarah Norman…. In the intervening six months between the accusation and the trial, however, Berry changed his mind and testified that he had lied, for which he was sentenced "to be whipte at the post." If Berry's original intention had been merely to smear Joanes, it is difficult to understand why he would do it in such a

In 1696, Mary Cox petitioned the Suffolk County Court of General Sessions of the Peace to show clemency for the "inadvertancy" of wearing men's clothing.

A Puritan heritage: The seventeenth century

way as to implicate himself. It is possible that the two men were lovers. Perhaps they had quarrelled, leading to the accusation, but later reconciled. Berry then decided to suffer the penalty for lying rather than have Joanes suffer the penalty for sodomy. Further evidence for this interpretation stems from a court order three years later when Joanes and Berry "and others with them" were required to "part theire uncivell liveing

together." Ten years later, one Richard Berry of Marshfield, a "grossly scandalouse person...formerly convicted of obsceane practises" was disenfranchised.[21]

Another possible network of relationships included John Allexander and Thomas Roberts, found guilty in 1636 of "lude and uncleane carriage one with another, by often spendinge their seede one upon another." In 1637, Thomas Roberts and three other men, including one Webb Adey, were brought before the court for "disorderly living" and required to explain their domestic arrangement. In 1640, Roberts was ordered by the court not to lodge with George Morrey, while Webb Adey was presented to a grand jury in 1641 for "licentious and disorderly manner of living."

An early-seventeenth-century network based on Plymouth Colony records

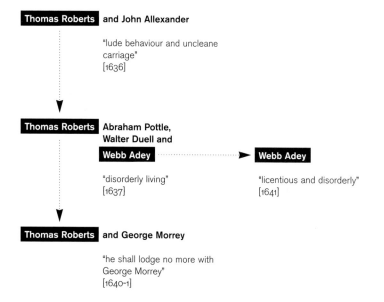

Thomas Roberts and John Allexander

"lude behaviour and uncleane carriage"
[1636]

Thomas Roberts Abraham Pottle, Walter Duell and

Webb Adey ····▶ **Webb Adey**

"disorderly living"
[1637]

"licentious and disorderly"
[1641]

Thomas Roberts and George Morrey

"he shall lodge no more with George Morrey"
[1640-1]

Sins of the flesh

Part of what differentiated Puritan categories of same-sex behavior from our own modern concepts of homosexuality was the absence of any notion of same-sex behavior as a distinct sexual identity. In Puritan New England, sodomy was seen as a sign of moral degeneracy, to which every "heart" was susceptible, rather than as a medical pathology or a preferred sexual orientation. Punishment was defended as a form of penance rather than treatment. Nonetheless, Puritan diaries and court documents reveal individuals who acted upon their unconventional desires.

O thou art full of Rottenness, of Sin within. Guilty…before God, of all the Sins that swarm and roar in the whole World at this Day, for God looks to the Heart, guilty thou art therefore of Heart-Whoredom, Heart-Sodomy, Heart-Blasphemy, Heart-Drunkeness, Heart-Buggery, Heart-Oppression, Heart-Idolatry.

Shepard was not above criticizing his own moral failings. In a passage from his autobiography, he describes an incident from his student days in England:

Title pages for *The Sincere Convert* by Thomas Shepard in English (left) and translated for Christian Indians (right)

"I went from him in shame and confusion"

Puritan minister Thomas Shepard (1605–1649) was born in England and reached Massachusetts in 1635; he assumed responsibility for the church at Newtown (Cambridge) the following year. An active and influential religious leader, Shepard was involved in conversion of the Indians and supervised the first Indian mission in Cambridge, established by John Eliot. He was tireless in his efforts to raise his congregation out of wickedness. One of his many published works, *The Sincere Convert* (1641), went through twenty-one editions; there, Shepard rails:

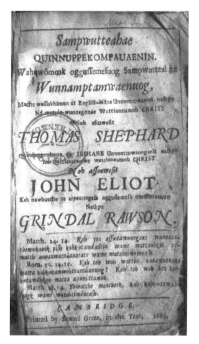

A Puritan heritage: The seventeenth century

Title page for the sixth edition of the poem *The Day of Doom* by Michael Wigglesworth

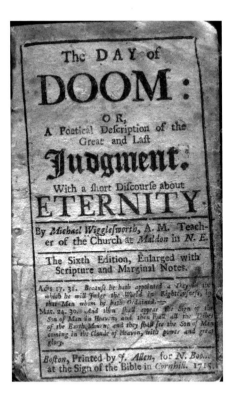

"Too much doting affection"

Michael Wigglesworth (1631–1705) became minister of the church in Malden in about 1656. His poem *The Day of Doom* (1662) was intended to prepare readers for judgment day; it was a colonial best-seller, with almost eighteen hundred copies purchased in the first year of publication. Wigglesworth had graduated from Harvard in 1651 and was appointed fellow and tutor, 1652–1654. In his diary, compromising sexual passages (shown italicized below) were written in a special shorthand code to conceal a deeply disturbing attraction for his students:

5 March 1653:
Too much doting affection *to some of my pupils, one of whom went to Boston with me today.*

5 April 1653:
Vain distracting thoughts molested me in my holy duties. *I find my spirit so exceedingly carried with love to my pupils that I can't tell how to take up my rest in God.*

4 July 1653:
Such filthy lust also flowing from my fond affection to my pupils whiles in their presence.

I drank so much one day that I was dead drunk, and that upon a Saturday night, and so was carried from the place I had drink at and did feast at unto a scholar's chamber, one Basset of Christ's College, and knew not where I was until I awakened late on that Sabbath and sick with my beastly carriage. And when I awakened I went from him in shame and confusion.

Another passage comments on this journal entry:

I was once or twice dead drunk and lived in unnatural uncleanesses not to be named and in speculative wantoness and filthiness with all sorts of persons which pleased my eye.[22]

At the advice of physician Dr. John Alcock, Wigglesworth married in 1655 and "by the will of God" consummated the union. The day after he confided in his diary:

I feel stirrings and strongly of my former distemper even after the use of marriage the next day which makes me exceeding afraid.[23]

Cotton Mather and the "Sins of Sodom"

A 1701 sermon by the Reverend Cotton Mather, "A Christian in his Personal Calling," makes a connection between the Puritan work ethic and the "Sins of Sodom." With the rational argument characteristic of the Puritan mind, Mather asserts:

Idle Gentlemen have done as much Hurt in the world, as *Idle Beggars*. And pardon me, if I say any *Honest Mechanics* really are more Honourable than Idle and Useless *men of Honour....* God hath placed us, as in a common Hive; Let there be no *Drone* in the *Hive....* The Sin of Sodom was, Abundance of Idleness. All the Sins of *Sodom* will abound, where Idleness is countenanced.[24]

Inspired by England's Societies for the Reformation of Manners, Mather launched a similar society in Boston to attack any perceived vice and immorality. His call to action appeared in the pamphlet *Methods and Motives for Societies to Suppress Disorders* (1702). Mather foresees a particularly pure city in the following passage:

Swearing and Cursing will not infect the Air; Men will not Reel along the Streets, by their Cups turned into Swine. The Cages of Unclean Birds will be dissipated. They whom Idleness renders Dead while they Live, will have an Honest Employment ordered for them, whereby they may Earn an honest Livelihood.

While English antivice organizations were responsible for the entrapment and execution of British homosexuals in the eighteenth century, no records exist to show that Mather's "Societies to Suppress Disorders" ensnared homosexuals in Boston. Mather's response to sexual and civil deviance took the form of the "voluntary association," in which nongovernmental organizations were responsible for monitoring private behavior.[25]

Title page of Cotton Mather's pamphlet *Methods and Motives*

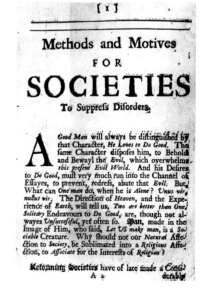

Coppy

New London October y:. 27. 1756

Whereas there has been a Rumour gone abroad in the World of my Bad Conduct or offencive Carriage towards Men in Bed. as far as I have been Guilty I am heartily Sorry and trust I have been heartily humbled before God for it and have Comfortable hopes I have obtained forgiveness And Dear Brethren and Christian friends With me in the Church I am heartily Sorry I have given you offence or grieved you and Desire your forgiveness With all Christians of What Denomi =nations Whatsoever and all that have known any thing that was Wrong in me I ask your forgiveness also. and all you my fellow Mankind in General I ask your forgiveness and I Cannot but commend the care of my Brethren at the General Meeting and their advice and admonition and heartily Submit unto it and ask forgiveness of you my Brethren I did not take their advice when come to me first from Swansey. And further I have to Say that I have given grounds of offence and Justify all the Church that took Such care to have Such things Repro =ved and Purged out of the Church This Confession from me

Stephen Gorton

this Confession has Been Read Publickly Sundry times to the Church and the 2d Sabboth day in April to the Church and World. Signed by us Whose names followeth ——— — - — Nehemiah Smith

David Latham

Boston in transition: The eighteenth century

Between 1689 and 1743, Boston's maritime trade made it one of the leading ports in the American colonies. The city landscape became a dense jumble of warehouses, wharfs, shops, public buildings, and homes. By 1743, 17,000 people lived on the small peninsula that was connected to the mainland by a narrow neck of land. These people increasingly came from different ethnic, religious, and social backgrounds; they made Boston a cosmopolitan urban center.

Although we have scattered references to homosexual activity in the eighteenth century, we do not have as clear a picture of this period as we do of either the seventeenth or the nineteenth century. A variety of social changes accounts for this disparity. There was a growing sense of privacy and a reluctance by civil authorities to pursue acts of immorality—especially among the upper classes. The rise of law as a profession contrasted with the communal scrutiny over personal lives characteristic of early Puritanism. Moreover, with the liberalized atmosphere of the evangelical revival of North America known as the Great Awakening, churches rather than civil authorities intervened in incidents of

sexual deviance; this "eldering" was often reported as a broad violation of the seventh commandment, which forbids adultery.[1]

Such was the case in two examples of homosexual behavior that have come to light from the study of eighteenth-century New England history in the Age of Enlightenment. In both instances, religious authorities seemed more concerned with institutional reputation than with interfering in private sexual behavior. In the case of the Reverend Stephen Gorton of the Baptist Church of New London and Lyme, the church intervened to stem a tide of public criticism and then restored him to his pastorate in 1757. Gorton was called to court for attempted sodomy; the charges were dismissed for lack of evidence. Ebenezer Knight of the Old North Church of Marblehead was suspended from Communion in 1732 for a "long series of uncleanness with mankind," but he was restored to membership six years later, after having earned the "charity" of the congregation.[2]

An epistolary romance

Although eighteenth-century women had little freedom to live independently, they formed passionate relationships with other women. Historians point to the invention of a self-conscious, idealized language of female friendship that blossomed from the late-eighteenth through the mid-nineteenth century. During the 1740s, the "heart" language of the Great Awakening, encouraged by evangelists such as Jonathan Edwards, allowed women to express love and intimacy. The twentieth-century tendency to view female relations in strict dichotomies of deviance/normality or erotic love/platonic love does not conform to the nature of women's emotional lives as revealed in diaries from the period.[3]

In the early 1750s, Sarah Prince, daughter of a Boston preacher, began a correspondence with Esther Edwards Burr, the daughter of the famous evangelist Jonathan Edwards and mother of the future vice president Aaron Burr. Although she admired and loved her husband, she also lived through periods of despair. Sarah Prince, who was unmarried, often chafed under the prospect of having to wed in order to participate fully in society. For seven years, the two women exchanged romantic letters and diaries full of sensibility and religious observation. Their correspondence is remarkable for its conflation of faith and passion, in which women burdened by domestic duty found mutual support and comfort. Burr, who referred to herself as "Burrissa" in affectionate parody of Samuel Richardson's literary heroine Clarissa, wrote to Prince on 8 February 1755:

What! These scrawls injoy the privilege of being handled in the most free and intimate manner and I deprived! In short I have good mind to seal up my self in the Letter and try if I cant Rival it.

On 15 February 1755, Burr wrote:

But to tell the truth when I speak of the world, and the things that are in the World, I dont mean friends, for friendship does not belong to the world. True friendship is first inkindled by a spark from Heaven, and heaven will never suffer it to go out, but I will burn to all Eternity.

On 4 June 1755, Burr responded to a letter no longer extant:

As you Say, I believe tis true that I love you too much, that is I am too fond of you, but I cant esteem and vallue too greatly, that is Sertain— Consider my friend how rare a thing tis to meet with such a friend as I have in my Fidelia.

On 12 April 1757, Burr reported that she had responded angrily to a Mr. Ewing, who had disparaged female friendship:

Mr Ewing says—she [poet Annis Boudinot] and the Stocktons are full of Talk about Friendship and society and such stuff—and made up a Mouth as if much disgusted—I asked what he would have them talk about—whether he chose they should talk about fashions and dress—he said things that they understood. He did not think women knew what Friendship was. They were hardly capable of anything so cool and rational as friendship.… I retorted several severe things upon him before he had time to speak again.

When Burr died in 1758, Prince recorded her loss:

The Beloved of my heart.… My whole prospects in this world are now changed. My whole dependence for comfort in the World are gone. She was dear to me as the apple of my Eye.… And she was mine! O the tenderness which tied our hearts! O the comfort I have enjoyed in her.[4]

Esther Edwards Burr

Boston in transition: The eighteenth century

Dandies, fops, bachelors, and *beaux*

Although historians sometimes assert that the association of effeminacy and homosexuality in Western culture is as recent as the 1895 Oscar Wilde trials, eighteenth-century rakes dressed effeminately—and Boston had its share of dandies. A newspaper of early-eighteenth-century Boston advertised the services of a popular George Brownell of Wing's Lane in 1713, who taught "Dancing, Treble Violin, Flute, Spinnet, &c. Also English Quilting and French Quilting, Imbroidery…and several other works."[5]

Sir Charles Hobby

"A gay man… of very different behavior"

Sir Charles Hobby (c. 1650–1715) was sent to England by the enemies of Joseph Dudley, governor of the Massachusetts Bay Colony, in the hope of soliciting the government to remove Dudley from office. One account describes Hobby as:

A gay man, a free liver and of very different behavior from what one would have expected should have recommended him to the clergy of New-England.[6]

He called it "Macaroni"

In the mid-eighteenth century, *Macaronis*—young men with long, curled hair, colorful clothes, and insatiable, omnisexual appetites—were a highly visible part of the London scene. Their outlandish behavior prompted denunciation, public ridicule, and, occasionally, timid emulation. Any dandy affecting a gaudy complement to his dress (like Yankee Doodle with his feather) was said to be doing so "à la Macaroni." Over time, the style spread to the colonies.[7]

"He surveys each person as he stalks the room"

This edition of the *Columbian Centinel and the Massachusetts Federalist,* dated 23 April 1800, describes one of the habitués of Boston's tavern society:

Antoinne, the French beau, has shaggy hair upon his head, which falls over his eyes and gives him the appearance of a hungry Buffalo. His neck is commonly muffled with a spotted linen kerchief; his wooly jacket painted with alternate streaks of yellow and black; while his green coat ends Behind in a mathematical point. He drinks *l'eau de vie* in the morning; talks about Parisian opera dancers on the exchange; sits at the dining table until dark. In female society his soul seems to recoil upon itself; and with gloomy caution he surveys each person as he stalks the room like a bear prowling around a sheep-fold.[8]

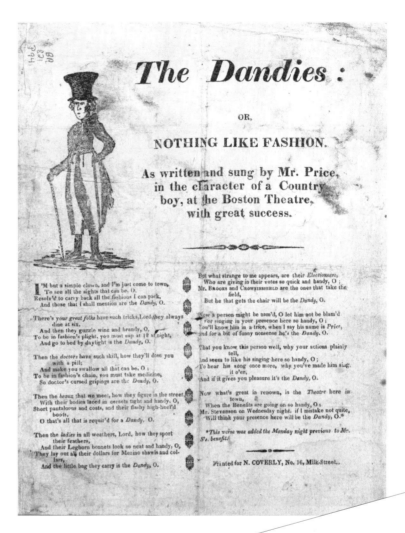

Above:
Early-nineteenth-century ballad

Right:
The *Columbian Centinel,*
23 April 1800

DEBORAH SAMPSON.
Published by H. Mann. 1797.

Above:
Frontispiece from 1797
biography of Deborah
Sampson by Herman
Mann

Right:
A Record Book entry
from the Massachusetts
Superior Court of Judica-
ture documenting the
case of the Government
and People v. Ann Bailey,
August 1777

Suff. ss. At the Superior court of Judicature, Court
of Assize, & General Goal delivery began & holden
at Boston within & for said county of Suffolk, on
the last tuesday of August Anno Domini Seventeen
hundred & Seventy Seven —

The Jurors for the Government and people of the
Massachusetts Bay in New England upon their oaths
present that Ann Bailey of Boston in the County of
Suffolk Spinster, fraudulently intending to cheat, and
infuse the inhabitants of this State, and of the united
States of America, did on the third day of March last
past at Boston aforesaid dress herself in man's apparel
to all parts of her body putting on the outward appearances of a young man; & there, & there falsely & deceitfully
presented herself to Abraham Hunt Esqr then & now
being a Captain, in the regiment of the united States of
America, whereof John Patterson Esqr was Colonel, and
pretended that She was a young man, and that her
name was Samuel Gay; & then, & there deceitfully offer-
to enlist herself into the service of the united States
of America in the company of the said Captain Hunt
as a young man, & into the station of a private Soldier, and that the said Ann Bailey then, & there fraudulently, & falsely, in consideration of being the
bounty given by this State to Soldiers enlisting into
the service of the united States of America, & also of
the bounty to be paid by said united States to Soldiers
so enlisting, enlisted herself as a young man, by the
name of Samuel Gay, into the service of the United
States aforesaid; and that the said Abraham Hunt giving credit to the pretensions aforesaid of the said
Ann Baily, & being deceived by her fraudulent dress,

Soldiers in disguise

Deborah Sampson

Disguised as a male, Deborah Sampson (1760–1827) enlisted in the Continental army in 1782 under the name of "Robert Shurtleff." Sampson fought in several battles and was wounded near Tarrytown, New York. Her true sex was discovered when she was hospitalized with a fever. Honorably discharged in 1783, Sampson returned to Massachusetts and married. For her Revolutionary War services, Deborah Sampson Gannett received pensions from the Commonwealth of Massachusetts and Congress.

Herman Mann, the author of Sampson's biography published in 1797, implied that Sampson had romantic liaisons with women while disguised as a soldier:

To mention the intercourse of our Heroine with her sex, would, like others more dangerous, require an apology I know not how to make. It must be supposed, she acted more from necessity, than a voluntary impulse of passion.

Some histories suggest that Deborah Sampson was an African American. William C. Nell includes the petition of Deborah Sampson Gannett to the

General Court of Massachusetts for compensation for wartime service in his *Colored Portraits of the American Revolution with Sketches of Several Distinguished Colored Persons* (1855).[9]

Ann Bailey

In August 1777 Ann Bailey was brought before the Superior Court of Judicature (now the Massachusetts Supreme Judicial Court) on a charge of fraudulently passing herself off as a man, using the name Samuel Gay, and enlisting in the Boston Regiment of Brigadier General John Patterson. Unlike Deborah Sampson, who became a hero as a result of her service, Bailey was arrested after her sex was discovered. Indicted by a grand jury, "Samuel Gay" Bailey pleaded guilty to the charges, was sentenced to two months in jail, and was ordered to pay a fine of sixteen pounds and court costs.

The 1777 Massachusetts Muster and Payrolls includes the following:

GAY, SAM. List of men mustered by Nathaniel Barber, Muster Master for Suffolk Co., dated Boston, Feb. 16, 1777; Capt. Hunt's co., Brig. Gen. Paterson's regt.

Friends and lovers

The late eighteenth and early nineteenth centuries reveal several notable examples of romantic same-sex friendships among Bostonians. These passionate, committed relationships, which sometimes lasted decades, often reached a level of intensity that equaled heterosexual marriage.

The soldier, the hairdresser, and the sailor

George Middleton was the leader of the Bucks of America, an all-black regiment during the American Revolution. Middleton and Louis Clapion, a French West Indian hairdresser, built the oldest standing house on Beacon Hill at 5 Pinckney Street. They lived together until 1792, when Clapion married and the house they shared was divided in two. Middleton never married, and his main friendships seem to have been with other men. When he died in 1815, he willed all his possessions to "my good friend Tristom Babcock," a mariner living on West Cedar Street.

Opposite:
The Middleton house,
5 Pinckney Street,
Beacon Hill

Below left:
George Middleton's will

Below:
The flag of the Bucks of America

Boston in transition: The eighteenth century

A romantic friendship

Boston-born Joseph Dennie (1768–1812) was educated at Harvard and maintained intense friendships with several college companions. Dennie was the editor of the *Port Folio* of Philadelphia, which was filled with discussions of friendship among men that were usually presented more favorably and desirably than relationships with women. His closest friend appears to have been Roger Vose (1763–1842).[10]

Right:
Silhouette of
Joseph Dennie

Opposite:
Letter from Roger Vose
to Joseph Dennie,
3 May 1790

Letter from Dennie to Vose, April 1790:

I have quite done with Castle building in the Air and endeavor to enjoy what I have.... The only wish I form is, that fortune, contenting herself with keeping us so long asunder, would now wheel about & suffer you to live & study with me at Groton. Depend upon it, Vose, so well acquainted am I with your disposition & my own, that united, we should enjoy as much felicity as this sublunary state can furnish. Would to God this scheme were practicable; and that for years to come one might be our table & one our bed. This topic can never be exhausted.

Letter from Vose to Dennie, 3 May 1790:

Castle building apart; let us consider the subject of profession a little more attentively. In case we should both study physic or divinity, we could doubtless agree on a place, and be covered each night with the same blanket. But let us extend our views a little farther. Let us take the most effectual method to lay the foundation for a permanent friendship.... A prospect of resting near Dennie for life would be very agreeable. Agreeable? It would be heavenly.

Cambridge, May 3. 1790.

Dear Friend,

Castle building apart; let us consider the subject of professions a little more attentively. In case we should both study physic or divinity, we could doubtless agree on a plan, and be covered each night with the same blanket. But let us extend our views a little farther. Let us take the most effectual method to lay the foundation for a permanent friendship. Compared with the ordinary term of life, three years are but a trifle. We must then look forward into life. A prospect of settling near Dennie for life would be very agreeable. Agreeable? It would be heavenly. Which, Dennie, on supposition we should follow the same profession, would more probably favour such a wish divinity or physic? Perhaps the latter. Yet, I imagine, friendship is commonly more ardent between neighbouring priests, than neighbouring physicians. This opinion is grounded on the supposition, that the interest of the latter is more apt to clash than that of the former. You will perhaps

The Anthologists

The *Monthly Anthology; or Magazine of Polite Literature* was first published in 1803. Many of its members were Harvard graduates who never married. The Anthology Society formally adopted a constitution in 1805 with Arthur Maynard Walter (1780–1807) as its first secretary. Shortly before the War of 1812, the *Anthology* ceased publication and reemerged as the *North American Review*. The Boston Athenæum was the offspring of the Anthology Society. The Anthologists relied on a network of close male friendships for emotional support, political identity, and personal confidence. Along with Walter, William Smith Shaw (1778–1826) and Joseph Stevens Buckminster (1784–1812) were at the core of this network of intense male friendships.[1]

A letter from Walter to Shaw, dated 19 December 1798:

I only want your cheering company to be completely happy. For your company, Shaw, by heavens, I would leave the conversation of half a dozen of the most beautiful creatures you ever saw. I can talk and laugh with these fine girls and enjoy exquisite heaven; but, Shaw, these are nothing to the luxuries I experienced at College.

Another letter from Walter to Shaw, 9 May 1799:

I long for the time to come, when I shall embrace you with the ardor of affection, when I shall tell you my plans of future life, and settle the sphere in which I am to move.

This journal excerpt, dated 26 November 1804, describes Walter's feelings for another member of the society, Benjamin Dana:

[Dana is] an almost friend.... I could easily make a friend of him.... He loves mystery & obscurity, which I abhor, and he doubts the existence of real friendship between man & man and thinks it only is between man & wife.

Portrait of Joseph Stevens Buckminster by Gilbert Stuart

This entry, dated 9 December 1804, mentions another acquaintance:

O I hope that he has the same feeling for me that I have for him…something of the tender, & something of the spirited in human life, which disposes me to be attracted towards him with something bordering on superior love.

Walter's death prompted the following eulogy from Buckminster:

Do you want examples of learned Christians? I could not recount them all in an age…. We have known and loved such men, and thank God, have been loved by them.

Above:
Portrait of William Smith
Shaw by Gilbert Stuart

Left:
The fourth volume of the
Monthly Anthology

Boston in transition: The eighteenth century

The Athens of America: The nineteenth century

By the 1820s, the United States was in the throes of industrial development, especially in New England, where small workshops of independent laborers were supplanted by mills and factories. Although the New England economy was still largely agrarian, textile mills began to dominate the landscape along the Blackstone, Connecticut, and Merrimack Rivers, signaling the onset of industrial capitalism in America.

These changes had a significant impact on American notions of class and gender. Industrialism produced a more complex system of social stratification than existed during the colonial period. The division of labor changed completely, as men left the fields to earn wages in nearby factories, and girls—who previously assisted their mothers in the home until marriage—increasingly did the same. A chasm developed between the girls of the mills and those of the middle and upper classes, who remained at home to learn the manners and morals of Victorian womanhood. As wage earners, men had the means to live independent of family, and bachelors of all classes could be found in the city. Among women, however, only the well-to-do could afford to live independently, or reside in a socially sanctioned "Boston marriage," a concept introduced to the reading public by Henry James in his 1886 novel *The Bostonians.*

It is difficult today to appreciate fully social conditions in the United States during the nineteenth century, when intimate relationships between people of the same sex were sanctioned and even encouraged. The separate spheres of men's "public" lives and women's "private" lives facilitated romantic attachments that had no taint of deviance ascribed to them. Such major figures as Emily Dickinson, Ralph Waldo Emerson, and Margaret Fuller glorified same-sex friendship, while Walt Whitman filled his poetry with robust imagery celebrating male "adhesiveness." Louisa May Alcott, the popular author of *Little Women,* extolled the virtues of intimate same-sex friendship in her 1870 novel *An Old-Fashioned Girl,* in which she describes the lives of two women artists:

Becky and [Lizzie] live together, and take care of each other in true Damon and Pythias style. The studio is their home—they work, eat, sleep, and live here, going halves in everything. They are all alone in the world, but as happy and independent as birds; real friends, whom nothing will part.

By the end of the century, however, masculine women and feminine men began to be considered deviant by medical authorities, and by "alienists" who specialized in abnormal psychology. Britain's 1895 sodomy trial of Oscar Wilde gave homosexuality a name, a face, and an "otherness" that served as the rationale for intense and oppressive public censure. The trial's influence was soon felt in America, where same-sex romantic friendships became suspect; in Boston, a number of confirmed bachelors rushed to marry. Same-sex relations, considered sinful during the colonial era, had become criminal by the end of the Victorian age.

The *Bachelors' Journal*

A bachelor's association published the above-mentioned journal in Boston, beginning in 1828. Reports in the *Bachelors' Journal* referred to similar organizations in Cambridge and Woburn. Typical for its time in the use of reprints, the journal contained travelogues, adventure stories, theater and literary reviews, humorous anecdotes, and poetry. The journal frequently argued for singlehood by itemizing the economic disaster of the married state.

On occasion the journal ridiculed dandies:

You'll find a well-bred cheat of fashion
Resolv'd through thick and thin
*   to dash on*
…
They cock'd their castors, twirl'd their
*   switches,*
Beat time on glassy boots and breeches,
With arms inlock'd they loung'd
*   the Mall,*
Look'd down on plebs, and took a stroll.

Other passages revealed a fascination with beautiful youths, as seen in this book review:

"Beautiful Boy at Play." N.P. Willis. This, bye the bye, has become a very fashionable subject. Boys are all the rage for poetry, while girls may go whistle for all that poesy cares for them. Here, however, is a good description of a boy's eyes:

And his dark eye's clear brilliance,
*   as it lay*
Beneath his lashes, like a drop of dew
Hid in the moss, stole out as covertly
As starlight from the edging of a cloud.

The main feature of the journal was the "Original Poetry" section on the back page of each issue. The poems usually bemoaned the pitfalls of heterosexual love, and praised the dignity of romantic friendship:

Friendship! sweet friendship, how dear is
*   thy name,*
When love and affection extend—
When the eye brightens with sympathy's
*   flame,*
While fann'd by the breath of a friend
…

Friendship! 'tis a title for love's young
dream,
On which the fond mind would depend—
While sailing down gently on life's wide
stream,
In search of a port and a friend.

The misogynistic tone of the *Bachelors' Journal* was of the "ball and chain" variety, which suggests that a portion of its readership would have been married men, called "Benedicks," or "Benedicts," in the journal. This may be an allusion to traitor Benedict Arnold, or to Shakespeare's character in *Much Ado about Nothing,* who, after forswearing marriage, finally succumbs to it.

THE BACHELORS' JOURNAL.

VOL. I.	THURSDAY EVENING, APRIL 24, 1828.	No. 1.

THE BACHELORS' JOURNAL *is published on Thursday of each week, by* SAMUEL G. ANDREWS, *No. 30, Market Street, Boston. Price $3, per annum, payable in advance.*

☞ *Persons paying for six papers, shall receive the seventh gratis.*

☞ *As this is the only paper in the Union devoted to the cause of Bachelors, it is hoped, and present appearances warrant the belief, that its circulation will be as extensive as the corps are numerous.*

☞ *Communications, post paid, must be directed to the Publisher.*

TO THE PUBLIC.

THIS is the first article in an editorial shape from the Bachelors' Journal; but be it especially understood that this is no criterion of what editorial articles hereinafter will be presented. In fact the beginning of a project, let the talents of its projector be however great, brings with it embarrassment to the individual presenter. Theories in their outset meet with scoffers, however practice may warrant their probability. Newton met with obstacles, and Franklin, when he first broached the doctrine of electricity, trembled as his pen approached paper to go abroad before a censorious world. But there is a firmness in mental energy, which can look the symptoms of defeat in the face, steadfastly, and be quelled only by fate. These observations, thrown out at random, apply in the case of the Bachelors' Journal.

There is in the city of Boston a vast deal of idle time, which, like the stream of some unknown island, runs to waste. It is unimproved for science, unoccupied by industry; and 'like the wild goose, goes unclaimed of any man.'—In married circles, the husband spends his leisure hours in domestic duties and cares—the married merchant finds the claims of his counting-house paramount to all others; but the single man, having a mine of leisure hours at his service, has 'no delight to pass away his time, unless to view his shadow in the sun, and descant on its quiet outlines—suffering his garden of intellect to be choked with weeds, for lack of an avenue whereby he can add to the stock of human literature. This is true; the past, the present, prove it. We ask the question of our younger and elder Bachelors if it be not so. Some have imagined, perhaps not without cause, from the very name of this paper, that it was to be one of the lighter sort and character—that it was to be a quiz. But it is not to be so. It is intended to be a vehicle for the research and intellect of the most gifted of the young, old, and middle aged of the corps of the single—and yet not to exclude those who have changed their state from Adam before the fall, to that of Adam and wife.

It is not pretended that this paper is to take the lead of modern journals, but it is openly stated that it will be entitled to a fair rank among the periodicals of the day, and it is avowed that the best talents of this city are pledged for its pages; and we may go further, and state that the Bachelors' Journal will concentrate some of the best energies of New-England. There is no promise of extensive patronage, but circumstances warrant the belief that its own merit will meet with its due reward. It ever has been that flatulent promises meet with but windy success; yet without promise, the thing of itself if it be good, finally receives its dues. It is not so much the subscriptions to the newspaper, (for so they call these things) that are wanted, as the intellects of the unmarried scientific. News can be obtained from any gossip—but real and true information must come from original conception, and accurate observation. The one is 'an old wife's story,' and the other, the Promethean scintillation of genius. But to end a concern which will be unique, vigorous, if we are not mistaken, and independent. In this we cannot be at fault; it may ... be entrusted in the hands of the young or old, of both single and double. Whether it be worthy of patronage, time alone can unfold. If not, let no one encourage it; if it be, the good sense of the community will bid us God speed. Under these circumstances the attention of our highest literary circles is requested, and the Bachelors of New-England must stand or fall in their literary reputation by the success of this, their proffered organ.

To the Publisher of the Bachelors' Journal.

DEAR SIR.—At this late period of my life spent so far in that dubious state of equivocal ease, called Bachelorship, I cannot but congratulate you upon your spirit in attempting to vindicate that cause, for which I have suffered, and in whose ranks I shall die.

Allow me to congratulate you and your corps for myself. I have no disobedient son—no unloving wife—no 'two cents for yeast' to distract me, and though loneliness dwells by my side in my cosy library, yet disquiet never protrudes itself from its pages. In fact, when evening comes, like a friend, in its calmness, into the window—when the sun like a Bachelor, quietly goes to bed, and wraps the bright clouds under his head for a pillow, it is then that the state of single blessedness is most dear to me. There is a comfort in disturbing the burning embers with the friendly poker—a delight in running over the events of the long past—and a quiet in pondering in dreamy speculation upon the future. True

it is, that no long train of relatives will follow us to the tomb—no hypocritical tears be shed, when the turf is sodded over my last home—and no outpourings of outrageous grief, at the reading of the will, which is to make or to mar the interested or disappointed. Yet still no less warm does my fire glow, and no less interest do my volumes afford, as the regular time for bed approaches, because of the lack of these posthumous honors, or crocodile tears. I know not how happy may be a matrimonial life—yet I know how peaceful is that of a Bachelor. The first, may be joyous, like the course of a stout bark over the waters, when heaven smiles and the seas in joyousness kiss its sides—the last, may be like that of some hermit upon his lonely isle, who wakes to pray, and who sleeps in peace—the former may meet with the varieties of storm, wreck and shine, and the latter may be doomed to a changeless tranquillity. The one may go down in horror, and the other deliberately hew out his grave under the bright willow, where the sun shall smile on it, in its moonlike gladness, and on which the moon, and fairies, and stars, delight to revel in nightly sport. The sojourner may shed a tear at the fate of the bark, and the anchorite be forgotten; yet as it respects both, to those individuals concerned, it amounts to the same result. They have passed away, and the coral and the turf alike conceal from mortal eye the victim.

But, my dear Sir, from your Journal, much is expected—not from us, who are without the pale of actual service in the cause of literature or public good, but from the squires, and younger knights, in the field of literary fame. Though our life be the most quiet, yet still our amount of good must be furnished to man. Charity looks with a keen eye to the unembarrassed, to the unemployed, and science makes us, in part, the holders of her torch. Obloquy should not make us morose, and contemplation should qualify us for good. When the storm beats upon our casement, the sorrows of others should be recollected, and when peace sits by our fire-side, then should be remembered the unhappiness of those who have embraced matrimony, instead of happiness. The sorrows of the fatherless will come to memory, when thought brings to reminiscence that which we owe to our mothers, and when we see the neglected sons of the unfortunate, let us remember our own disabilities in younger days, when we looked upon a wife as the consummation of our fondest wish. But the garrulity of an old man, has led him to a long article, when he intended only to have said a few things by way of encouragement to you in your project, even as a wood-cutter sometimes hews up a whole tree, when he calculated only to have felled it.

Yours, &c.   ICHABOD.

First issue of the
Bachelors' Journal,
24 April 1828

Romantic friendship, fraternal love

The separate spheres of men's and women's lives that evolved in the late eighteenth and early nineteenth centuries provided opportunities for both men and women to develop intimate relationships with members of the same sex. The female world of friendship was much more extensive than that developed by men. Two things in particular limited the opportunities for men to be affectionate with each other. First, society believed that self-restraint was an important aspect of masculinity. This meant that intimate relationships between men could always fall under suspicion for being too close. Second, too much intimacy was not only seen as unnatural—it was also equated with sodomitical behavior.

Despite these restraints, some men discovered ways of circumventing the barriers of masculinity. One such means was through the cult of "special friendships." This cult seems to have developed as classical Greek writings trickled into schools for middle- and upper-class boys. The examples of Damon and Pythias and Orestes and Pylades presented a model of intimate, loving same-sex friendships between males.[1]

"The fountains of my hidden life"

Ralph Waldo Emerson (1803-1882) was one of the most influential American thinkers of the nineteenth century; as an essayist, poet, and lecturer, he philosophized about the relationship between man and God, and was a leader of the transcendental movement. As a student at Harvard, Emerson's attention was drawn to a young scholar, Martin Gay:

There is a strange face in the Freshman class whom I should like to know very much. He has a great deal of character in his features & should [be] a fast friend or a bitter enemy. His name is Gay. I shall endeavor to become acquainted with him & wish if possible that I might be able to recall at a future period the singular sensations which his presence produced at this.

Though he later excised portions of the text, Emerson's 1821 journal is full of statements of affection for Gay, as well as a "memory sketch" portrait. Gay "haunted" Emerson's thoughts for over two years. In 1822 Emerson wrote, "It is with difficulty that I can now recall those sensations of vivid pleasure which his presence was wont to waken spontaneously." The lesson of this special bond was clearly reflected in his mature writings.[2]

Me too thy nobleness has taught
To master my despair;
The fountains of my hidden life
Are through thy friendship fair.[3]

Ralph Waldo Emerson (above) developed a passionate attachment to his Harvard classmate Martin Gay. Emerson filled his 1821 journal with statements about his affection for Gay, as well as this "memory sketch" portrait (right).

"Two sturdy oaks"

Henry David Thoreau (1817–1862), the author of *Walden,* took Emerson's lofty model of platonic love as his own. He used this model to explain the emotional attraction he felt for certain men who came into his life, like the Canadian woodcutter Alek Therian, whom Thoreau would encounter in his walks around Walden Pond. Whatever physical attraction Thoreau might have felt toward men could not be openly proclaimed. In his poem "Friendship" he expressed the inexpressible:

Henry David Thoreau

Two sturdy oaks I mean,
*   which side by side,*
Withstand the winter's storm,
And spite of wind and tide,
Grow up the meadow's pride,
For both are strong.

Above they barely touch, but undermined
Down to their deepest source,
Admiring you shall find
Their roots are intertwined
Insep'rably.[4]

In the summer of 1839, Thoreau was smitten by the young brother of a family friend, Edmund Sewall, who was in Concord for a visit. The love poem—"Lately, Alas I Knew a Gentle Boy"—written to the object of his affection is remarkable for its candor:

So was I taken unawares by this,
I quite forgot my homage to confess;
Yet now am forced to know,
*   though hard it is*
I might have loved him
*   had I loved him less.*[5]

Rejected love

One of the great literary friendships of the nineteenth century was that shared by New England writers Herman Melville (1819–1891) and Nathaniel Hawthorne (1804–1864). On 5 August 1850, the two met at a picnic in Stockbridge, Massachusetts. When a sudden thunderstorm came up, they were forced to seek shelter among the rocks of Monument Mountain; the two hours spent alone in conversation sealed their relationship. Melville, the younger man, immediately formed "a reckless emotional attachment" to the forty-six-year-old Hawthorne, a father figure but, "more than handsome, so darkly gorgeous."[6]

Hawthorne was very reserved; indeed, his wife claimed that he hated to be touched. After visiting the Shaker community at Hancock, New Hampshire, Hawthorne wrote in his notebook how shocked he was to find the male members of the celibate sect sharing narrow cots:

Their utter and systematic lack of privacy, their close conjunction of man with man, and supervision of one man over another—it is hateful and disgusting to think of.[7]

Nathaniel Hawthorne

Naturally, the attentions paid by Hawthorne's ardent new friend were troubling, and the fifteen months they spent as neighbors in Pittsfield were psychologically intense for both men. Melville (who also had a wife), was devastated as Hawthorne grew distant from him. Most scholars agree that Melville's "Monody" is really an elegy to Hawthorne, summing up his grief over love rejected:

To have known him, to have loved him
After loneness long;
And then to be estranged in life,
And neither in the wrong;
And now for death to set his seal—
Ease me, a little ease, my song![8]

Herman Melville

"He would die for me"

Melville's tales of men at sea were based on actual experience. In Polynesia, he witnessed societies where homosexuality was an accepted part of life. In *Moby Dick* (1851), which he dedicated to Hawthorne, Melville describes the interaction between the South Seas islander Queequeg and the Yankee sailor Ishmael, who share a bed one night at New Bedford's fictitious Spouter Inn:

> Upon waking next morning about daylight, I found Queequeg's arm thrown over me in the most loving and affectionate manner. You had almost thought I had been his wife.

Ishmael grows ever closer to the "Pagan," and the following day they undergo a ritual bonding:

> When our smoke was over, he pressed his forehead against mine, clasped me 'round the waist, and said that henceforth we were married; meaning, in his country's phrase, that we were bosom friends; he would die for me, if need should be.

As one scholar has written, "Melville had an unfailing eye for handsome men." In lush prose Melville describes the beauty of characters like the Polynesian Marnoo in *Typee* and the blond sailor, Billy Budd, who causes general commotion among the entire crew of the *Indomitable.* Melville distinguished between the base conduct of men spending months alone at sea, and the spiritual love between men (and women) that was Emerson's ideal. It is the wedding of souls that Melville depicts in his epic poem "Clarel"—a depiction of Melville's urgent need for intimacy with Hawthorne. Suddenly overtaken by love for the attractive Vine (a thinly disguised portrait of Hawthorne), the younger Clarel gushes,

O, now but for communion true
And close; let go each alien theme;
Give me thyself![9]

A mystic thrill

The Boston transcendentalist Margaret Fuller (1810–1850), a friend and protégée of Ralph Waldo Emerson, was one of the most brilliant and scholarly American women of the period, and certainly the first to theorize on the subject of same-sex relationships. While living in Jamaica Plain, she wrote a revolutionary feminist work titled *Woman in the Nineteenth Century* (1845), in which she states, "The growth of Man is two-fold, masculine and feminine," meaning that everyone possessed both masculine and feminine qualities.

Emerson's assessment of Fuller was that she had "what in woman is generally called a masculine mind"; other contemporaries commented freely on her unladylike assertiveness. Fuller's relationship with her young cousin, Anna Barker, was described by one historian as "Margaret's most cherished romantic love." Even in an age where strong emotional attachments between women were commonplace, the depth of Fuller's sentiments was extraordinary. After Anna Barker's marriage in 1840, Fuller reminisced:

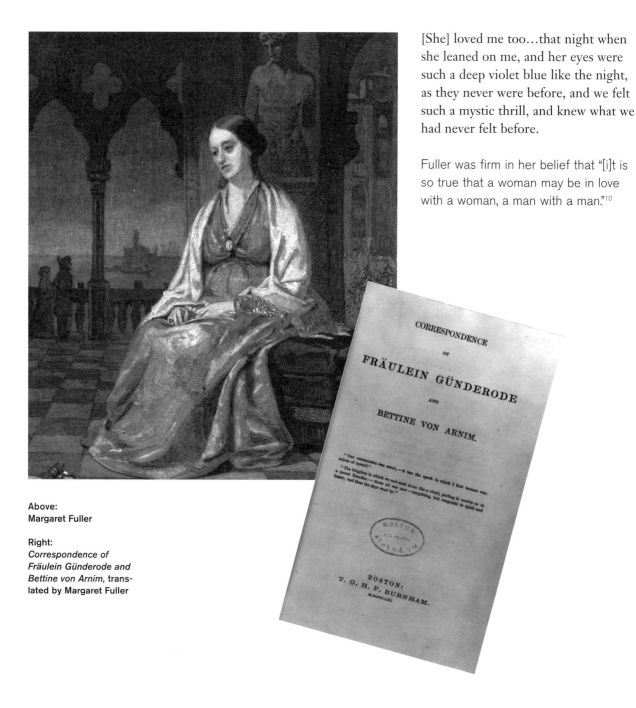

[She] loved me too…that night when she leaned on me, and her eyes were such a deep violet blue like the night, as they never were before, and we felt such a mystic thrill, and knew what we had never felt before.

Fuller was firm in her belief that "[i]t is so true that a woman may be in love with a woman, a man with a man."[10]

Above:
Margaret Fuller

Right:
Correspondence of Fräulein Günderode and Bettine von Arnim, translated by Margaret Fuller

"My Bride had slipped away"

Margaret Fuller's 1842 translation of the correspondence between Karoline Günderode and Bettine von Arnim, two German writers who had loved each other at the beginning of the century, was the inspiration for many of the letters and poems written by Emily Dickinson (1830–1886) of Amherst to her friend Sue Gilbert. After Gilbert's marriage to Austin (Dickinson's brother), Emily fell in love with Sue's school friend, Kate Scott. Their romance lasted for a number of years, culminating in the summer of 1860, when they spent a night together. Emily commemorated this event in one of her poems (c. 1862) to Kate, describing it as a symbolic marriage:

Her sweet Weight on my Heart a Night
Had scarcely deigned to lie—
When, stirring, for Belief's delight,
My Bride had slipped away—[11]

Emily Dickinson

215

"Every leaf but the fig leaf"

The poetry of Walt Whitman (1819–1892) contained images linking emotional, spiritual, and physical love between men, distinguishing it from the lofty platonic sentiments of earlier American writers. Bostonian Edward Everett Hale greeted Whitman's *Leaves of Grass* (1855) with words of praise in the *North American Review,* though others had reservations.

Emerson quoted Edwin Percy Whipple's remark that *Leaves of Grass* "had every leaf but the fig leaf," but he sent Whitman a complimentary letter upon its publication, writing, "I greet you at the beginning of a great career." Whitman had learned from Emerson that a man could accept and celebrate himself in cosmic language, but the masculine, affectionate, contemplative, and sensual tone of Whitman's poetry shocked many. When Whitman appeared in Boston during March 1860, Emerson attempted to persuade him to tone down or delete from *Leaves of Grass* the passages involving sexuality. In fact, the Boston Brahmin elite, led by journalist and editor Thomas Wentworth Higginson, were disgusted by Whitman and in 1882 had *Leaves of Grass* declared obscene. Other, more liberal-minded Bostonians, such as Katharine Lee Bates, formed a local branch of the International Walt Whitman Fellowship.

When Walt Whitman (left) arrived in Boston in March 1860, Ralph Waldo Emerson registered him for guest privileges at the Boston Athenæum (above).

Top:
Leverett Saltonstall (1825–1895, right) sitting next to his Harvard class-mate Charles William Dabney Jr. and an unidentified friend, c. 1850. Saltonstall traveled with Dabney after graduation and generally had a difficult time settling down; it was said that he was forced by his mother, against his will, to marry.

Bottom:
George Barrell Emerson, educational leader (1797–1881, right), and Samuel Joseph May (1797–1871), Unitarian clergyman, abolitionist, and reformer, graduated from Harvard together in 1817. Though both married, they maintained an intimate friendship for their entire lives.

The Athens of America: The nineteenth century

Charles William Dabney Jr. (top row, left) with officers of the Massachusetts Forty-fourth Volunteer Regiment

An "exquisite" soldier

In *Memoranda During the War,* Whitman wrote of his heart-wrenching experiences in Washington, D.C., as a nurse tending wounded Union and Confederate soldiers. While life in military service meant adherence to the manly virtues of loyalty, courage, and strength, more refined qualities in soldiers were also deemed worthy of praise. Charles William Dabney Jr. of West Roxbury was admired for the "exquisite and almost feminine gentleness of his bearing."[12]

Expressions of love between men in uniform were common in the correspondence and literature of the period. In Bostonian Fred W. Loring's novel, *Two College Friends* (1871), his characters, Tom ("soft curling brown hair, deep blue eyes and dazzling complexion") and Ned ("the complexion is olive, the eyes brown, the lips strongly cut"), fall in love in school and eventually go off to war together. In a torrid scene at the novel's end, Ned visits Tom, who is lying wounded in a military hospital:

O my darling, my darling, my darling! please hear me. The only one I have ever loved at all, the only one who has ever loved me.... O Tom, my darling! don't forget it. If you knew how I love you, how I have loved you in all my jealous morbid moods, in all my exacting selfishness, —O Tom! my darling, my darling!

The Athens of America: The nineteenth century

Nathan Appleton Jr. (1843–1906), proudly photographed in the fashionable costumes he wore playing "Emily (a nice young woman in a predicament)" in the 1862 all-male Harvard Hasty Pudding Club production of "Grimshaw, Bagshaw, & Bradshaw." After graduating in 1863, Appleton was appointed second lieutenant in the Fifth Massachusetts Battery, and was wounded the following year in the battle of Virginia Central Railroad.

A contradictory life

While studying at Harvard's divinity school, Thomas Wentworth Higginson forged a romantic friendship with a younger student, William Henry Hurlburt (1827–1895). This relationship, according to Higginson's wife and biographer, was a loving one, though it was mysteriously "destined to end in sorrow." Documented in a series of letters "more like those between man and woman than between two men," Higginson, in response to a question about his friendship with Hurlburt, describes it as follows:

But I never loved but one male friend with a passion—and for him my love had no bounds—all that my natural fastidiousness and cautious reserve kept from others I poured on him; to say that I would have died for him was nothing. I lived for him; it was easy to do it, for there never was but one such person.... To me, moreover, he was always noble and sweet, he loved me truly and generously.[13]

Thomas Wentworth Higginson (1823–1911) as commanding officer of the first African American regiment in the Union army, the First South Carolina Volunteers

Higginson led a full, fascinating, and, in some ways, contradictory life. A reformer, he espoused women's suffrage and was ardent in his opposition to slavery. He is said to have "discovered" Emily Dickinson and was the first to publish her work. Yet, despite his friendship with William Henry Hurlburt and all that meant to him, he was Walt Whitman's fiercest Boston critic.

The Athens of America: The nineteenth century

Damon and Pythias

In 1866, the painter Winslow Homer (1836–1910) sailed from Boston on the *Africa* for Europe. Homer spent a year in Paris, where he shared a studio in Montmartre with his friend from Belmont, Albert Warren Kelsey (1840–1921). Although Kelsey inscribed the back of this photograph "Damon and Pythias," alluding to the loving youths of Greek mythology, he seems in later years to have rejected his sojourn with Homer as a frivolous interlude.[14]

**Winslow Homer (seated)
and Albert Warren Kelsey**

Charlotte's web

Toward the middle of the nineteenth century, a group of highly mobile, independent women began enjoying an international, transatlantic lifestyle that now seems strikingly modern. These women were respected members of the art world, earned large incomes, and kept company with the intellectual and moneyed elites of the time. Actress Charlotte Cushman (1816–1876) was the most visible and influential of these women.

Cushman set up a feminist household in Rome in the 1850s. Born in Boston's North End, she debuted in New Orleans during 1836 as Lady Macbeth. A versatile actor, Cushman played comic as well as tragic parts, and appeared in more than thirty male roles, a fact that caused public comment. "Tall, with a convincing masculine stride, deep voice, and strong features, she showed to advantage in a doublet" as Romeo. As an international celebrity, she maintained a house in London and wintered in Rome; her apartment on the Via Gregoriana became a mecca for theater people and aspiring artists. She announced her retirement from the stage in 1852, but continued to give "farewell" performances until 1874. She died of breast cancer in 1876.[15]

The Athens of America: The nineteenth century

Left:
Throughout the years, Cushman's maid and companion was Sallie Mercer.

Right:
Florence (Florrie) Freeman (1836–1883), an aspiring Boston sculptor, went to Rome in 1861. She was put under the care of Charlotte Cushman. Her hair is cropped boyishly short as a defense against marble dust.

Sculptor Emma Stebbins (1815–1882) left New York for Rome in 1857 and immediately fell in with a talented young artist, Harriet Hosmer, who had first come to Rome with Charlotte Cushman five years earlier. According to her most recent biographer, Cushman's tumultuous decade-long relationship with British writer and translator Matilda Hays suffered its final blow when Cushman became enamored with Stebbins.[16]

By the time they returned from an Easter excursion to Naples, Charlotte and Emma knew they would plan their lives together. They donned black bowler hats for daily rides to the Borghese.[17]

Once Cushman and Stebbins became involved, Cushman's loyalty to her partner led her to promote Stebbins's career over that of Hosmer, her former protégée. Stebbins eventually followed Cushman back to the United States, where they set up households in Newport and Boston.

Above left:
Charlotte Cushman
(seated) and Matilda
Hays

Left:
Emma Stebbins

Above:
Charlotte Cushman
(right) and Emma Crow,
another member of
Cushman's household

The Athens of America: The nineteenth century

Right:
Harriet Hosmer in her Rome studio, at work on a statue of Missouri senator Thomas Hart Benton, 1865

Below:
Grace Greenwood (the pen name of Sara Jane Lippincott, 1823–1904) was a popular writer and a champion of the anti-slavery and women's rights movements. She wrote in 1850, "Thank Heaven woman herself… is beginning to feel, and to cast off, the bonds which oppress her—many of them, indeed, self-imposed…but none the less bonds."[18]

"A Harem (Scarem) of emancipated females"

Born in Watertown, Harriet Goodhue Hosmer (1830–1908) was raised by a permissive father who gave her "horse, dog, gun and boat," and encouraged her to lead an active life out-of-doors. She quickly developed into an "incorrigible tomboy."

She arrived in Rome in 1852 and lived for a time in Charlotte Cushman's household. William Wetmore Story, writing to his Boston friend, poet James Russell Lowell, observed that Cushman, Hosmer, Matilda Hays, and

writer Grace Greenwood formed "a Harem (Scarem) of emancipated females." While many American visitors appreciated Hosmer's growing talent as a sculptor, others were shocked by her unfeminine appearance and manners, and by her flamboyant behavior—she was criticized for riding about the countryside on horseback, unescorted. Story wrote to his wife, after a visit to Hosmer's studio:

Miss Hosmer's want of modesty is enough to disgust a dog. She has had casts for the entire [nude] model made and exhibited them in a shocking indecent manner to all the young artists who called upon her. This is going it rather strong.

Her success as an artist led to rumors by jealous male rivals that her work was not her own. She nonetheless made her own way through life as the first woman to support herself as a sculptor in the nineteenth century.[19]

Harriet Hosmer and her workshop assistants at her Rome studio, 1861

Lewis's 1874 statue of Hygeia, the Greek goddess of health, was commissioned by Dr. Harriot K. Hunt for her grave in Mount Auburn Cemetery, Cambridge. Hunt was the first woman physician in Boston.

Edmonia Lewis

Born of mixed West Indian and Native American (Chippewa) heritage, Edmonia Lewis (1844?–c. 1911) attended Oberlin College, the first coeducational and interracial college in the United States. She went on to Boston, where she hired a room in the Studio Building on Tremont Street and took lessons in sculpting from Anne Whitney. Lewis soon garnered the support of influential abolitionists such as William Lloyd Garrison and Elizabeth Palmer Peabody. She went on to produce portraits of John Brown, Garrison, and other abolitionists, as well as a bust of Henry Wadsworth Longfellow.

The sale of one hundred plaster copies of her portrait bust of Colonel Robert Gould Shaw (the commanding officer of the black Massachusetts Fifty-fourth Regiment) enabled Lewis to relocate to Rome in 1865; there she was welcomed by Charlotte Cushman, Harriet Hosmer, and their circle. Lewis emulated both the outward attributes of their unconventional, often masculine attire, as well as their aesthetic independence. In an interview in the *New York Times,* 29 December 1878, Lewis stated:

I was practically driven to Rome in order to obtain the opportunities for art-culture, and to find a social atmosphere where I was not constantly reminded of my color. The land of liberty had no room for a colored sculptor.

Using the struggle of peoples of color as her theme, she was the first African American sculptor to win an international reputation.[20]

The Athens of America: The nineteenth century

Spinsters and tomboys

"Mary Casal" (her real name is not known) was born in western Massachusetts in 1864. Her autobiography, *The Stone Wall,* published in 1930, is the amazing psychosexual self-portrait of a young woman's growing awareness and acceptance of her lesbian identity. For a time, she taught in "a very select girls' day school on Beacon Hill" and is quite possibly included in the photograph of Miss Ireland's school (below).

The students and teachers of Miss Catherine I. Ireland's private school at 92 Mt. Vernon Street on Beacon Hill (1887), where a generation of girls from Boston's best families were educated. Standing in the doorway in a plumed hat is Elizabeth Brewster Ely.

Sex-segregated secondary schooling allowed many young women to share in a variety of social, cultural, and recreational pursuits. Administrators of women's colleges in the Boston area—which provided a home away from home for girls of the upper classes—encouraged the formation of close bonds between students. In some cases, these adolescent relationships developed into permanent domestic partnerships. Living outside of marriage was not possible economically for many women, but some single women of the upper classes were able to form positive identities around their status as spinsters, and informal networks of women companions sprang up. For women who preferred not to marry, spinsterhood could provide the framework for a fulfilling life.

One such network was documented in an article entitled "Lynn Spinsters' Party" in the *Lynn Item* of 5 June 1896:

Something new in the way of parties was given Thursday afternoon by Mrs. Harriet Purrington. A social event that was something of a novelty at her home at 831 Western Avenue, a party where no gentlemen were admitted and married ladies were prominent for their absence—

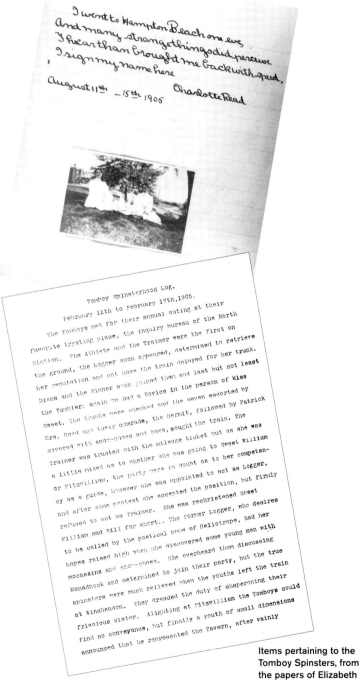

although a few of the latter were allowed to hover around the outer circle of the company.

Over one hundred spinsters attended the party. One feature of the event was a poem delivered by Miss J. E. Roach:

O Muse of Spinsterdom, this song inspire
And help me sing with true poetic fire
The praises of that noble sisterhood,
So oft by married folk misunderstood
...
The married folk have had their holiday,
For bachelors and maids
  let's all make way.
The rulers of the world the spinsters
  shall be,
The spinsters, calm, serene of spirit, free.
I ask you, "Is not this the coming she?"

The trainer, the tumbler, the athlete, and the novice

Elizabeth Brewster Ely preserved the papers of the Tomboy Spinsters, a club that was active at the turn of the century. Members of this sisterhood went on hiking expeditions in the White Mountains, where they would be given nicknames such as The Trainer, The Tumbler, The Athlete, and The Novice, or on visits to the Ely summer home in Manchester, "Dame Cottage."

Items pertaining to the Tomboy Spinsters, from the papers of Elizabeth Brewster Ely

Being together

During the 1800s, a great number of new educational institutions, female-dominated workplaces, and social organizations appeared. Massachusetts women moved away from parental homes to work in the Lowell textile mills and Lynn shoe factories. Women of privilege began attending women's colleges such as Wellesley, Radcliffe, Simmons, Wheaton, and Mount Holyoke. Others organized settlement houses, joined women's clubs and unions, or became members of utopian communities. The advent of these institutions represented the first time in U.S. history that women were encouraged to be independent, and to explore the public and private pleasures of being together.[21]

A smashing romance

Women's colleges clearly encouraged close bonding. In an 1873 letter, a student described a ritual called "smashing":

When a girl takes a shine to another, she straightaway enters upon a regular course of bouquet sendings, interspersed with tinted notes, mysterious packages of "Ridley's Mixed Candies," locks of hair perhaps, and many other tender tokens, until at last the object of her attentions is captured, the two become inseparable, and the aggressor is considered by her circle of acquaintances as "smashed."

From another letter:

If the "smash" is mutual, they monopolize each other and "spoon" continually, and if it isn't mutual, the unrequited one cries herself sick and endures pangs unspeakable.

After 1875, according to one scholar, such passionate relationships between young women were increasingly seen as abnormal by the medical and psychiatric community.[22]

An excerpt from the poem "My Sophomore," by Alice Welch Kellogg, class of 1894, published in *Wellesley Lyrics* (1896):

There is a Wellesley sophomore bright,
As fair as a maid can be;
And in the lore of the days of yore
There are few so skilled as she.
But oh! the grace of her winsome face
Is more than her learnèd mind;
And to all, I own, save poor me alone,
Most gracious she is and kind.

Two Simmons College undergraduates at the seashore near the turn of the century

The Athens of America: The nineteenth century

The drawing room of the
house that Annie Adams
Fields (at window)
shared with Sarah Orne
Jewett at 148 Charles
Street, Beacon Hill

"There were, in my parents' circle of friends in Boston, several households consisting of two ladies, living sweetly and devotedly together. Such an alliance I was brought up to hear called a 'Boston marriage.' Such a 'marriage' existed between Mrs. Fields and Sarah Orne Jewett. Father wrote of it as a 'union— there is no truer word for it.'"

Helen Howe, *The Gentle Americans: Biography of a Breed* (1965)

Boston marriages

**Carla Wenkebach and
Margarethe Müller,
members of the
Wellesley German
department, during
the 1890s**

**Margaret Pollock
Sherwood and Martha
Hale Shackford, also
members of the
Wellesley College
faculty**

In the latter part of the nineteenth century, adult women involved in long-term relationships were regarded by contemporaries as having a kind of marriage. In fact, Bostonians as late as the 1960s used the term *Boston marriage* to describe this phenomenon. The women who entered into these relationships referred to themselves as spinsters, celibate women, or women involved in a romantic friendship; many today would probably identify themselves, or be identified, as lesbians.

Of course, only those women who had professional careers or who inherited money could possibly afford to live outside of the traditional family. At Wellesley College, which opened in 1875, a number of the mostly female faculty paired off into committed relationships that combined career and personal life and came to be called "Wellesley marriages."

Inseparable

The relationship between Alice James (1848–1892) and Katharine Peabody Loring (1839–1943) was one of the most celebrated Boston marriages. Alice, the sister of Harvard psychologist William James and novelist Henry James, was of a frail constitution. She first met Katharine Loring in 1873; by 1879 the two were inseparable. Katharine Loring was everything to Alice James, according to one of her biographers—"man and woman, father and mother, nurse and protector, intellectual partner and friend." Of his sister's relationship with Loring, Henry James wrote: "A devotion so perfect and generous…was a gift so rare…that to brush it aside would be almost an act of impiety." In Alice and Katharine, James found a model for the feminist characters in *The Bostonians* (1886).[23]

Alice James (reclining) and Katharine Loring, taken at the Royal Leamington Spa (England), c.1890

Annie Adams Fields

Sarah Orne Jewett

"Your dear love holds me close to you"

The Boston marriage of James's and Loring's close friends, Sarah Orne Jewett (1849–1909) and Annie Adams Fields (1834–1915), was similarly idealized. Fields's diaries were used by M. A. DeWolfe Howe in his 1922 publication *Memories of a Hostess.* When her husband, the publisher James T. Fields, died in 1881, Howe notes that Annie's "need…for an absorbing affectionate intimacy was met through her friendship with Sarah Orne Jewett." Jewett was a regionalist writer, inspired by New England characters and themes. In 1875, the *Atlantic Monthly* published a poem by her that explains, in Howe's words, "the union— there is no truer word for it—that came later to exist between herself and Mrs. Fields":

And when the busy day is done
And work is ended, voices cease,
When every one has said good night,
In fading firelight, then in peace

I idly rest: you come to me,—
Your dear love holds me close to you.
If I could see you face to face
It would not be more sweet
*   and true.*

"O beautiful"

Katharine Lee Bates was born in Falmouth in 1859 and attended Wellesley College. There she met Katharine Coman, commencing a twenty-five-year relationship that ended with Coman's death in 1915. Bates became a respected member of the English faculty and a published poet; the words for "America the Beautiful" were inspired by a trip she made to Pikes Peak, Colorado. Less well known was her collection of poems *Yellow Clover: A Book of Remembrance* (1922), dedicated to the memory of her partner, Katharine Coman. Publication of these poems inspired notes of appreciation to Bates for her having captured "a woman's love for a woman."

In a letter sent to Coman from London in 1891, Bates writes:

For I am coming back to you, my Dearest, whether I come back to Wellesley or not. You are always in my heart and in my longings. I've been so homesick for you on this side of the ocean and yet so still and happy in the memory and consciousness of you.[24]

Katharine Lee Bates, lyricist of "America the Beautiful"

YELLOW CLOVER

A Book of Remembrance

BY

KATHARINE LEE BATES
AUTHOR OF "FAIRY GOLD,"
"THE RETINUE," ETC.

Katharine Coman

The Athens of America: The nineteenth century

74 The eminent sculptor
Anne Whitney
(1821–1915), who had
known Charlotte
Cushman and her circle
of women artists in Rome
during the 1860s, was an
early advocate of Negro
and women's rights.
She is shown (seated),
c. 1885, with her lifelong
companion, the painter
Abby Adeline Manning
(1835–1904).

"You melt my strength"

The flamboyant, cigar-smoking Amy Lowell (1874–1925) was directly responsible for helping to modernize American poetry. Lowell first met the divorced actress Ada Dwyer Russell in 1909, and in 1912 the two began a successful courtship. Two years later, they were living together in Lowell's Brookline mansion. Much of Lowell's poetry alludes to their loving relationship. This passage is from "The Wheel of the Sun":

In the street,
You spread a brightness where you walk,
And I see your lifting silks
And rejoice;
But I cannot look up to your face.
You melt my strength,
And set my knees to trembling.
Shadow yourself that I may love you,
For it is too great a pain.

Amy Lowell

Above:
Gertrude Stein (1874–1946) as a student at the Harvard Annex, which became Radcliffe College in 1894

Opposite left:
Angelina Weld Grimké

Opposite right:
Vida Scudder (left) and Florence Converse

"They were very regularly gay"

Born in Pennsylvania and raised in California, Gertrude Stein studied at Radcliffe in her early twenties under William James and George Santayana. She moved to Paris in 1903, where she was an influential writer and renowned patron of the arts, and where she lived in an expatriate Boston marriage with Alice B. Toklas. Her elliptical style of writing is clearly reflected in a passage from her short story "Miss Furr and Miss Skeene":

They were quite regularly gay there, Helen Furr and Georgine Skeene, they were regularly gay there where they were gay. They were very regularly gay. To be regularly gay was to do every day the gay thing that they did every day. They were regularly gay.

"My heart overflows with love"

Angelina Weld Grimké (1880–1958) was born into a distinguished biracial Boston family and attended several liberal upper-class schools, including Carleton Academy in Ashburnham; she was assisted in receiving a superior education by her white great-aunt, Angelina Grimké Weld, who had been a prominent abolitionist. She graduated from the Boston Normal School of Gymnastics in 1902 and, from 1906 to 1910, attended summer classes at Harvard. She then became a teacher.

At Dunbar High School in Washington, D.C., Grimké and her fellow teacher, Mamie Burrill, fell madly in love. In a letter to Grimké, Burrill writes:

Could I just come to meet thee once more, in the old sweet way, just coming at your calling, and like an angel bending o'er you breathe into your ear, "I love you."

Grimké writes back:

Oh Mamie if you only knew how my heart overflows with love for you and how it yearns and pants for one glimpse of your lovely face.
    Your passionate lover

As a poet, Grimké was later associated with the Harlem Renaissance movement of the 1920s. A portion of her poem "El Beso" (The Kiss) reads:

Your mouth
And madness, madness
Tremulous, breathless, flaming,
The space of a sigh.[25]

"Her comrade...and companion"

Vida Scudder (1861–1954) graduated from Smith College and accepted a position in the English department at Wellesley. Her concern over "privilege unshared" led her to socialism. She became a founder and guiding force behind Denison House, one of Boston's first settlement houses. In 1919, writer Florence Converse (1871–1967) joined Scudder's household and, until Scudder's death, was her "most intimate friend, her comrade in radical causes and companion in the deepest spiritual experiences."[26]

The Athens of America: The nineteenth century

78 Edith Guerrier (seated, left) and her classmates from the Vermont Methodist Seminary and Female College, Montpelier, c. 1888. In later years, Guerrier and her partner, Edith Brown, worked with immigrant girls in Boston's North End and West End neighborhoods.

A tale of two Ediths

The granddaughter of an abolitionist, Edith Guerrier (1870–1958) inherited her grandmother's urge to work for social welfare. Arriving in Boston in 1892, she secured a position in the nursery of the North Bennet Street Industrial School in the North End, and by 1899 she was managing the boys' and girls' reading rooms at the West End branch of the Boston Public Library. She then organized story-hour groups for high school girls, which became the Saturday Evening Girls Literary Club.

While taking an evening course at the Museum School, Edith Guerrier met another student, "a pretty young thing, shy as a fawn," named Edith Brown. They began taking walks together, and soon were a couple. Edith Brown taught drawing at North Bennet Street and in 1908 became director of the pottery studio. In 1915, backed by phil-anthropist Helen Osborne Storrow, Guerrier and Brown built a two-story workshop on top of Nottingham Hill in Brighton, where the Paul Revere Pottery was established and where the two women lived until Brown's death in 1932.[27]

Edith Guerrier and Edith Brown at Nottingham Hill

Edith Guerrier in later life

The Athens of America: The nineteenth century

"A booster and an S. E. G."

This piece is taken from *S. E. G.* [Saturday Evening Girls] *News: The Official Library Clubhouse Paper,* 13 December 1919:

Who is Sylvia?
  And what is she?
Sylvia B. is a booster
  And an S. E. G.

The following took place at the library a short time ago:

The Saturday Evening Girls Literary Club was formed by librarian Edith Guerrier, c. 1910.

(*Enter Sylvia. F. is busy at the shelves. F. turns.*)

"[F.] Good evening, Sylvia.
S. Good evening. (All in one breath) Say, Fanny, you are looking fine tonight.
F. (Blushing) Oh, Sylvia, what's the joke?
S. Why no joke at all. I've been standing here for some minutes and simply couldn't take my eyes off you. I've been watching you and thinking that if I were a man I would propose to you. Why should we wait until one is dead to say nice things about them. If we only got more "boosts" and less "knocks" in life we'd be so much happier. I believe in complimenting the living. If you have any flowers or sweet things for or about me let me have them now when I can enjoy them, and don't wait for my funeral."

You are quite right, Sylvia. We all agree with you for this is good logic.
S. E. G. no more knocks. Open the door and come right in with the boosts.

Creating a female dominion

By the latter part of the nineteenth century, many of the women graduating from colleges like Smith, Wellesley, Simmons, and Mount Holyoke were seeking more tangible opportunities to reform society than those available through traditional venues, such as the women's club movement. Urban conditions were severe, and Boston's North, West, and South Ends in particular were economically impoverished immigrant ghettos. Women professors at Boston-area colleges encouraged their students to enter public life after receiving their degrees, and to exercise civic responsibility by working to uplift the poor. Social service became the means for privileged women to become closely involved with the lives of less fortunate women. In the process, they created a "female dominion" separate from the spheres of commerce, industry, and government controlled by men.[28]

The settlement movement began in London in 1884. In 1889 Jane Addams bought a residence on the West Side of Chicago that became known as Hull House. Boston's South End House opened in 1891, and Denison House, on Tyler Street, the following year. Settlement houses were set up to provide neighborhood services and support to individuals and families and to teach skills to recent immigrants. This was accomplished through friendship clubs, handicraft classes, language instruction, hobby groups, and practical skills training.

Peabody House settlement and gardens in Boston's West End

The Athens of America: The nineteenth century

Dr. Dimock

Susan Dimock (1847–1875) was born in Washington, D.C., and attended Washington Academy, where her study of Latin led to her interest in learning medicine. In 1864, Dimock and her widowed mother moved to Sterling, Massachusetts, in order to be near relatives, and then they relocated to

Susan Dimock

Hopkinton, where Dimock studied medical texts provided by a woman doctor through Bessie Greene, the daughter of Boston reformer and anarchist William Batchelder Greene. In 1866 Dimock entered the New England Hospital for Women and Children as a student. Harvard Medical School refused her admission, however, and the lack of opportunity for advanced training in medicine forced her to go to Europe. In 1872, she returned to Boston's New England Hospital as one of the most highly qualified of the early women doctors. There she professionalized the nation's first nursing school, where the country's first African American nurse, Mary Eliza Mahoney, had been trained.

On a sabbatical in 1875, Dimock, Bessie Greene, and another friend boarded a steamship in New York bound for Europe. Off the coast of England, the ship was wrecked; Dimock, Greene, and nearly all on board were killed. Describing her relationship with Greene, Dimock's biographer wrote, "They were lovely in their lives, and in death they were not divided."[29]

A Nobel cause

Born in Jamaica Plain, Emily Greene Balch (1867–1961) was a student at Miss Ireland's school on Beacon Hill. Rather than attend the Harvard Annex (Radcliffe), she and her classmate Alice Bache Gould entered Bryn Mawr College in Pennsylvania, where Balch took a degree in economics. Returning to Boston in 1892 to attend a summer seminar, she fell in with Katharine Coman and Vida Scudder of Wellesley College, and began her teaching career at Wellesley as Coman's assistant. She was deeply involved with the social reform movement and was a founder of Denison House in Boston's South End. A pacifist and civil libertar-

ian, Balch believed strongly in the tenets of Quakerism and established the Women's International League for Peace and Freedom. She was awarded the Nobel Peace Prize in 1946.

For many years, she shared a house in Wellesley with Agnes Perkins of the college's English department and Perkins's friend Etta Herr; they were eventually joined by Mabel Cummings. In 1904 Balch wrote in her diary:

I have just read a note from a friend who loves me. It is strange that a woman can love me but a man cannot.... I am happy as an unmarried woman.[30]

Top:
Group portrait, possibly of the founders and staff of Denison House, c. 1896. Emily Greene Balch is seated left of the little girl.

Above:
Emily Greene Balch (left) at a luncheon in 1931 with social reformer Jane Addams

The Athens of America: The nineteenth century

Bohemian Boston

Caricature of Oscar Wilde as the Bard of Beauty, c. 1890

Bohemianism, an underground urban lifestyle characterized by emancipation from the family and its values and constraints, had its origin in the Paris of the 1840s, where this youthful subculture was organized around cafés. Soon most major European and North American cities had pockets of artists and writers leading creative but highly unconventional lives. By the 1880s, the aesthetic philosophy of English writer Oscar Wilde began to exert a profound influence in Boston on a group known as the Visionists. Wilde's first American tour in 1882 was a sensational affair. When he came to Boston to lecture on the Pre-Raphaelites, Harvard students threatened to pay homage to Wilde by attending his lecture in "dress coat, knee breeches and silk stockings, with lilies in their buttonholes."[31]

The Visionists

Part of Wilde's attraction for the Boston bohemians, who were centered around architect Ralph Adams Cram (1863–1942), was his passionate belief in "art for art's sake" and in the nobility of artistic production over all other activities. Prominent Visionists included photographer F. Holland Day (1864-1933) who, with his friend Herbert Copeland, started a publishing company that printed the first American edition of *The Yellow Book* (the avant-garde British arts journal), as well as Wilde's *Salomé* and other sexually provocative texts from England. Publication of *Salomé* in 1894 completely shocked genteel society, and the book was immediately withdrawn from circulation by the Boston Public Library. Day was a highly regarded artistic innovator. In 1895 his Pinckney Street studio witnessed the first public exhibition in Boston of a photographic male nude—a study for the Crucifixion.

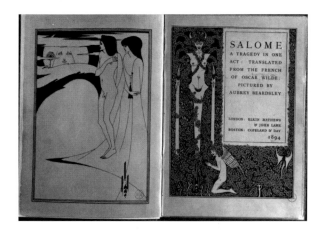

Wilde's *Salomé,* with illustrations by Aubrey Beardsley, published by Copeland & Day in 1894

Above:
A "medieval" dinner party
at the Day mansion,
c. 1893. Day is standing
at the end of the table.

Left:
Visionists Copeland,
Guiney, Cram, and Brown
on the veranda of the
Day mansion in Norwood
(1892)

The Athens of America: The nineteenth century

Right above:
Codman family and friends at "The Grange," Lincoln, Mass., c. 1895. Seated, Thomas Newbold Codman (left) and Ogden Codman (right)

Right:
Frontispiece and title page for *The Decadent*

Below:
Daniel Berkeley Updike (left) and Ogden Codman (right)

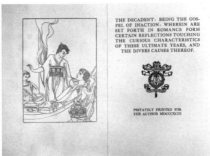

Right:
Codman's bookplate, printed by Updike

"A queer sort of place"

Ralph Adams Cram's novel *The Decadent: Being the Gospel of Inaction* was published in 1894. Describing the hidden world of bohemian Boston in a "decrepit and degenerate age," the book was published anonymously "in order to elude local apprehensions about the Visionists and their late-night carousing, smoking, drinking, and carrying on." Nevertheless, Cram wrote:

In some way…word got abroad that [ours] was a queer sort of place; and in certain more conservative circles this did no good to our budding reputations.[32]

Types

Like Copeland and Day, Daniel Berkeley Updike (1860–1941) was inspired by the aesthetic movement to found his own printing firm, the Merrymount Press, named after Thomas Morton's seventeenth-century colony. His two-volume *Printing Types: Their History, Forms, and Use* is still in print. Interior designer Ogden Codman (1863–1951) had many clients in high society and, with novelist Edith Wharton, wrote *Decoration of Houses* (1897). His brother, Thomas Newbold

Codman (1868–1963), was a music critic and amateur photographer whose papers include a notable collection of male erotica.[33]

Guiney and Brown

Though the Visionists were primarily a society of men, their ranks included Irish American poet and literary scholar Louise Imogen Guiney (1861-1920) and writer Alice Brown (1856-1948). Guiney, whose research on the English Romantic poets was greatly respected, was a driving force behind Boston's Aesthetic movement of the 1890s. She enjoyed a friendship with Brown of which many, including F. Holland Day (Brown's neighbor on Beacon Hill) were jealous. In her affectionate biography of "Lou," Alice Brown reminisces:

You could hardly imagine her, at any age, without her girl's grace, her mystic smile. A long-legged romp in petticoats far beyond the milestones when childhood is apt to slink away abashed before oncoming desires and dignities, she was early in love with the sweet seclusion of books and equally with gay adventure out of doors.

Guiney (left) and Brown in walking costume during their 1895 tour of England, where they went to write a travel sketch for a Boston women's organization

The Athens of America: The nineteenth century

Day's photographic studies, mostly inspired by classical mythology, featured young waifs encountered on the streets of the South End. His most famous protégé was a young Lebanese boy living with his family on Tyler Street, near Denison House. Kahlil Gibran (1883–1931) went on to fame as the author of *The Prophet*.

African Americans served as models in a number of Day's groundbreaking photographic studies. "Ebony and Ivory" (1898) was described as "one of the first pictures taken in the United States that ennobled a black American."[34]

Vagabondia

The popular *Vagabondia* series was a poetic collaboration between the Canadian-born poet Bliss Carman (1861–1929), Richard Hovey, and designer Tom Meteyard. Carman, "tall, blond, handsome and rather flamboyant," was the link between bohemian Boston and Harvard, where he had come to study, falling under the influence of philosopher George Santayana (1863-1952). Homosexual themes figured prominently in the work and life of the Madrid-born and Boston-bred Santayana, who studied and taught at Harvard in the 1880s and 1890s.[35]

Purple ink

The Cult of the Purple Rose: A Phase of Harvard Life, published in 1902, is a satire commenting on the influence of the aesthetic movement on Harvard undergraduates during the 1890s. The author, Shirley Everton Johnson (1871–1911), describes the genesis of the cult in the words of one of the founders:

"Oh, it will be simply lovely," he said, "and so original! We will all wear purple roses, and write on purple linen…use three-cent purple stamps instead of the customary twos, and if any of us should ever write on white paper, he must invariably use purple ink. Besides, we would attract so much attention with our purple handkerchiefs and hat ribands. It will be so gratifying to hear people remark on how hideous they are, and we can be as truly happy as the end and aim of art will allow."

Left:
Bliss Carman

Below:
Shirley Everton Johnson

The Athens of America: The nineteenth century

Mrs. Jack

Isabella Stewart Gardner (1840–1924) was a legend in her own time. Starting with the untimely death of her husband, John Lowell Gardner, in 1898, his widow, called Mrs. Jack, embarked on an ambitious program of art acquisition which culminated in the transformation of her fabulous Venetian-style palazzo, Fenway Court, into a beloved cultural institution. She accomplished this feat largely by relying on the skills, expertise and companionship of the coterie of attractive and talented homosexual men—mostly artists, collectors, and curators—that she gathered around her. Born in New York and always considered an outsider by the Brahmin elite, Mrs. Jack held extremely progressive social views, and supported the aspirations of Asians, Jews, African Americans, and Italian and Irish immigrants—groups that were beginning to challenge the Yankee hegemony in Boston.

Above:
Isabella Stewart Gardner at Eastern Point with Henry Davis Sleeper (second from left) and A. Piatt Andrew Jr. (far right), c. 1909.

Left:
Henry Davis Sleeper (left) and A. Piatt Andrew Jr., November 1914, at Gloucester. Sleeper's frail constitution prevented him from participating in the rough-and-tumble games and amusements favored by Andrew and his young male friends—mostly Harvard undergraduates.

Society painter

By 1908 Mrs. Jack's circle included the society painter John Singer Sargent (1856–1925). Born in Italy to American parents, Sargent had first come to Boston in 1887. After a solo exhibition in 1888 at the St. Botolph Club, he was commissioned in 1890 to design murals for the new Boston Public Library in Copley Square. Along with other commissions—for the Museum of Fine Arts and Harvard's Widener Library—Sargent was almost fully occupied in Boston for the next twenty-five years. While circumspect about his private life, an album of male nudes that Sargent, a bachelor, kept for his own enjoyment offers insight into his predilections.[36]

Left:
Male nude by John
Singer Sargent

Above:
Isabella Stewart Gardner
(covering her face) and
John Singer Sargent

The Athens of America: The nineteenth century

This snapshot of a party at Eastern Point shows Cecilia Beaux (top right) with A. Piatt Andrew Jr. (lower left) and Henry Davis Sleeper (second from left).

Seaside shenanigans

In the years preceding World War I, Isabella Stewart Gardner, John Singer Sargent, and others in their circle were drawn into the wealthy summer enclave at Eastern Point, Gloucester, where Harvard professor (later U.S. congressman) A. Piatt Andrew Jr. (1873–1936) and his neighbor, interior designer Henry Davis Sleeper (1878–1934), had homes. The letters from Sleeper to Andrew provide evidence of the intensity of his feelings.[37]

Social life on Eastern Point revolved around ceaseless entertaining. One of Gardner's biographers hints at the goings-on at Andrew's home, Red Roof: "Gossip had it that often all the guests were men, their pastimes peculiar. Yet all the ladies on Eastern Point were fascinated by Piatt." Portrait painter Cecilia Beaux (1863–1942) spent summers at her Gloucester home, Green Alley, where she enjoyed hosting evening gatherings of her neighbors. She never married. "Faithful in attendance were Harry Sleeper and Piatt Andrew, whose brilliancy of repartee has never been excelled," according to an observer. Concealment and ambiguity characterized the lives of many of the women and men who moved through this exclusive world of polite manners and material luxury.[38]

Left:
Attic black-figure kylix, attributed to the Amasis Painter, c. 555-525 B.C., Museum of Fine Arts, Boston. This piece is part of the collection of Greek, Etruscan, and Roman erotic art given by Ned Warren to the museum in 1908, but not officially accessioned and cataloged until the 1950s, when it was finally made available for public viewing.

Uranian love

Born in 1860, Edward Perry "Ned" Warren grew up on Beacon Hill; he was a sensitive boy who loved art and music, typically running around in a toga while his brothers were playing Indians. He hated Boston. A family-owned paper mill provided Ned with the means to travel in Europe and to indulge his pleasure in beautiful things. Leaving Harvard, he entered Oxford University and began a lifelong study of ancient Greek civilization, embarking on a remarkable quest to bring the artistic treasures of that civilization to the United States.

In 1890 he established at Lewes House, in England, a "brotherhood" of similarly-minded gay men, who for the next thirty years gathered antiquities from all over Europe—marble sculpture, pottery, and bronzes. With his lover, John Marshall, Warren built the classical antiquities collections at Boston's Museum of Fine Arts and at the Metropolitan Museum of Art in New York.

Warren, also a writer, was influenced by the philosophy of Walter Pater and John Addington Symonds, who pursued an aesthetic ideal derived from the classical celebration of same-sex love and worship of male beauty. Using the pseudonym Arthur Lyon Raile, Warren produced what he considered his magnum opus—a three-volume study of man-boy love based on the Greek model—*A Defense of Uranian Love* (1928–30) ("Uranian" is a term derived from Plato's *Symposium*). Ned Warren died in 1928. His ashes were brought to Italy to be interred next to Marshall's in the English Cemetery at Bagni di Lucca.[39]

Above:
Edward Perry Warren in his early thirties

Silk pajamas

A denizen of Beacon Street in the Back Bay, Charles Hammond Gibson (1874–1954) was a minor poet and author. A frequent guest at Henry Davis Sleeper's estate, Beauport, he also regarded himself as a designer. For a time, he served as Boston Parks Commissioner and was responsible for the architecture of the Beaux Arts–style "comfort station" on the Boston Common. His own home has been preserved as a shrine to late-Victorian taste and style. Gibson, who employed a series of young, working-class men as his live-in servants, was said to have upset his prudish neighbors by appearing about the neighborhood in silk pajamas.[40]

Above:
Charles Hammond Gibson (seated at the desk) with author John P. Marquand

Left:
Thomas Russell Sullivan

The club scene

The membership of Boston's artistic and literary clubs—the St. Botolph Club (1879), the Tavern Club (1884), and the Club of Odd Volumes (1887)—was derived principally from Harvard graduates who wanted to maintain the ties they developed in the school's social clubs and fraternities. These private men's dining clubs also served as safe and convivial spaces where well-to-do gay members of Boston's cultural establishment could express themselves freely and creatively. The Tavern Club, which had a distinct bohemian aura about it, counted a number of members from Mrs. Jack's circle, including George Santayana; librarian Theodore Dwight; musicians Charles Loeffler and Tymoteusz Adamowski; and Thomas Russell Sullivan. Tavern Club theatricals, directly descended from the cross-dressing antics of the Hasty Pudding Club, were legendary.[41]

Top:
The inner sanctum of the Tavern Club, c. 1909. The inscriptions on the wall read (above), "Here We Come To Unbend," and below, "Wine Wit Music Wisdom Friendship Poetry Youth Weed."

Above:
The "Dancing Girls" from the Hasty Pudding Club's Spring 1901 production, "The Dynamiters"

The Athens of America: The nineteenth century

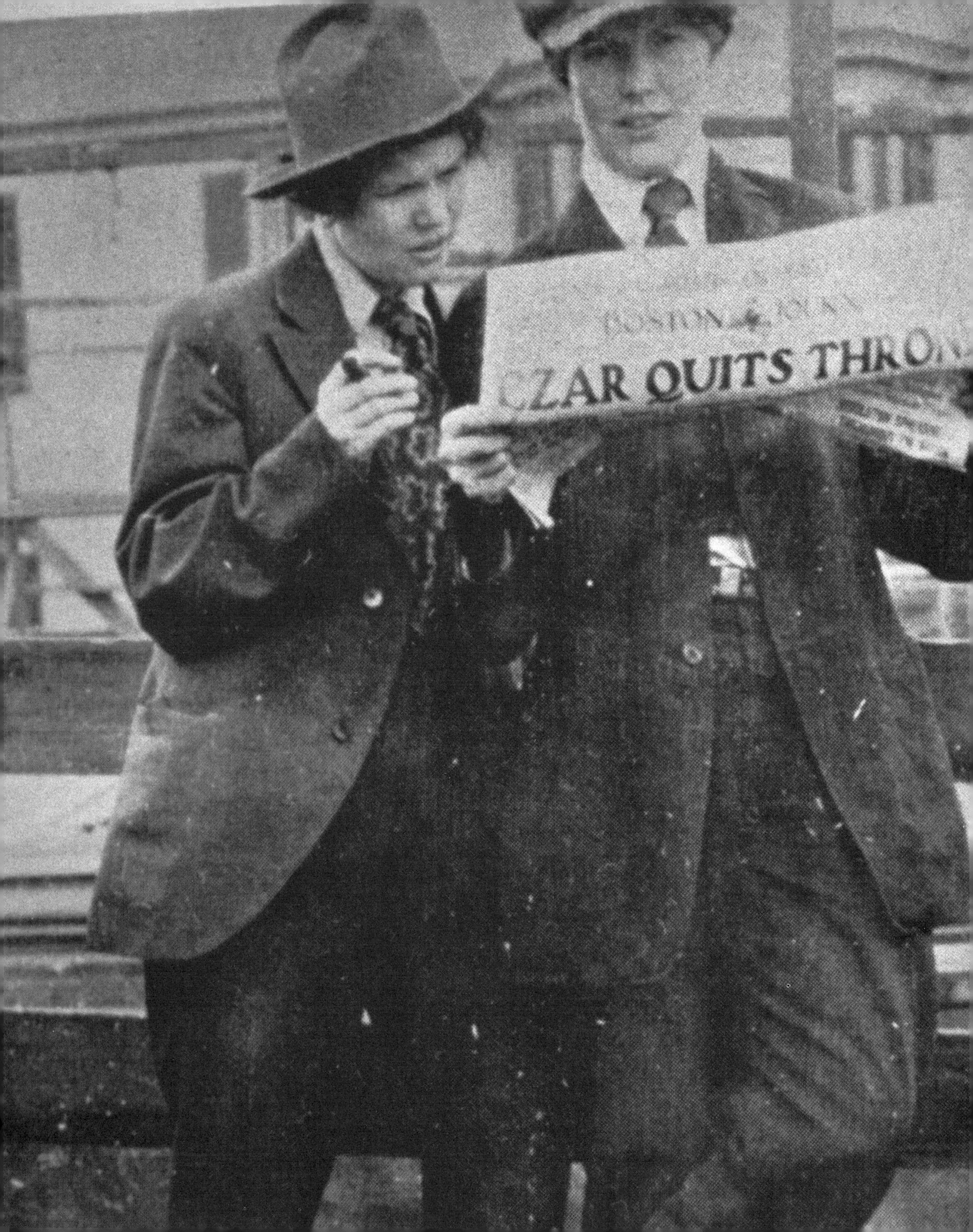
CZAR QUITS THRO

"It was Cæsar who first started men to wearing earrings. Why shouldn't men wear them now? The girls wear their hair like men do, therefore it wouldn't make much difference in looks. I, for one man, am in favor of men also wearing earrings. I would like to know if there are other men who also want to wear earrings.... I myself have worn earrings many evenings while out for a walk. —MR. F. RICKER"

From a letter to the editor of the *Boston Traveler* (25 July 1931)

Opposite:
Passing women, 1917

The early twentieth century: 1900–1945

By 1900, industrialization had begun to effect profound social and demographic changes in American culture. During the nineteenth century, men and women of all social classes had often lived separate lives; some were even able to carry on committed same-sex relationships without public accusations of deviance. As the new century began, however, what the Victorians had called the "separate spheres" of the sexes began to disintegrate, as more and more women entered the paid labor force. These working women, like European immigrants and the blacks migrating to northern cities, were simultaneously accused of destabilizing the home and threatening the social order. Deep cultural anxieties about masculinity and femininity emerged as a barrage of commentators responded to what many saw as the demise of proper social and sexual "hygiene" among Americans.[1]

The 1920s marked the first time that the majority of America's people lived in cities. Factory workers, discharged draftees, displaced farmers, and immigrants all discovered the freedom that came from being on their own, away from parental control and the expectations of their closely knit communities. Urban gathering places, such as cafés and taverns, provided opportunities for independent people to meet and socialize—including those with so-called deviant tendencies.

Deviations from gender and sexual norms entered the realm of medical analysis during the early twentieth century through the work of sexologists and other researchers. As a result, theories pertaining to homosexual behavior, which were often manipulated to promote a preconceived moral or social agenda, emerged as a discrete area of specialization within psychoanalytic theory and practice. By mid-century, these specialists would be called upon to commit punitive acts against homosexuals in the service of governmental institutions, such as the U.S. military, which relied on these "authorities" to brand thousands of homosexuals as unfit.[2]

Understandably, these developments had a chilling effect on the ways in which homosexuals perceived themselves as individuals and members of the community. As lesbians, gay men, bisexuals, and transgendered people began to gather in communities, they also needed to ensure that their new subcultures remained virtually invisible to the general public. Otherwise, they risked persecution by police, city officials, and self-appointed authorities such as the New England Watch and Ward Society and the Catholic Church's League of Decency. Those caught violating laws that forbade certain sexual acts, loitering, or cross-dressing risked the loss of job, home, and family, if not imprisonment or confinement in a mental institution.

Given this atmosphere, it is hardly surprising that much of our information about "deviant" life in the years leading up to the conclusion of World War II comes from often lurid newspaper stories, court records, and the archives of religious groups and regulatory boards. These sources, even as they document the existence of homosexual communities, attest to their constant oppression.

This section of *Improper Bostonians* examines the research of twentieth-century sexologists, male and female cross-dressing, censorship, and the years encompassing World War II.

A new category

In the late nineteenth and early twentieth centuries, researchers in Germany and England originated ideas that would have a profound impact on how society viewed homosexuals. (The first known use of the word *homosexual* was by Dr. Karoly Maria Benkert in 1869, who was arguing for the decriminalization of German sodomy laws.) These researchers, who came to be known as sexologists, developed new terms to describe patterns of sexual behavior they observed, particularly homosexual behavior.

Many of these researchers were themselves homosexual. The German sexologist Karl Heinrich Ulrichs used the term *Uranian* to describe a "female soul" trapped in a male body. The physician Magnus Hirschfeld, leader of the first homosexual emancipation organization, used the term *third sex* to describe a person having sexual characteristics of both genders. (Hirschfeld was later murdered by the Nazis, who also destroyed the research institute he founded.)

The British sexual liberationist Edward Carpenter, an early supporter of the women's movement, thought of himself as a member of an "intermediate sex," a syndrome that he viewed as having positive implications for society's view of changing sex roles. John Addington Symonds described a "color blindness" of sexual instinct. Havelock Ellis, who believed in biological determinism, introduced the word *invert,* and popularized the use of the word *homosexual* in the English language. (Ellis felt that the women's movement was responsible for both an increase in lesbianism and the breakdown of the traditional family unit.)

Other members of the psychoanalytic community had much more negative views of homosexuality. German physician and neurologist Richard von Krafft-Ebing presented the theory that homosexuality was a mental abnormality in his *Psychopathia Sexualis.* During the 1920s, Sigmund Freud cited improper child rearing as the cause of homosexuality and prescribed psychoanalytic therapy as its cure. This view of the homosexual as neurotic was central to Freud's ideas, which soon became dominant and contributed greatly to the subsequent oppression of homosexuals.[3]

"How many homosexuals I've come to know!"

Magnus Hirschfeld reprinted this letter from an anonymous Bostonian, written several years before, in a 1914 edition of the *Monthly Reports of the Scientific-Humanitarian Committee.* It is interesting to note how the writer quite comfortably uses such relatively new terms as *homosexual, bisexual,* and *Uranian* to describe the members of his subculture:

I'm always delighted to hear about even the smallest success you have in vanquishing deep-rooted prejudices. And here in the United States we really need this kind of activity. In the face of Anglo-American hypocrisy, however, there is at present no chance that any man of science would have enough wisdom and courage to remove the veil which covers homosexuality in this country. And how many homosexuals I've come to know! Boston, this good old Puritan city, has them by the hundreds. The largest percentage, in my experience, comes from the Yankees of Massachusetts and Maine, or from New Hampshire; French Canadians are also well represented.

Here, as in Germany, homosexuality extends throughout all classes, from the slums of the North End to the

The early twentieth century: 1900–1945

highly fashionable Back Bay. Reliable homosexuals have told me names that reach into the highest circles of Boston, New York, and Washington, D.C., names which have left me speechless with astonishment. I have also noticed that bisexuality must be rather widespread. But I'll admit that I'm rather skeptical when homosexual friends say that they're far more attracted by the female sex. I'm often amused by someone assuring me of his bisexuality and later meeting him where there are no women.

There is astonishing ignorance among the Uranians I've come to know about their own true nature. This is probably a result of absolute silence and intolerance, which have never advanced real morality at any time or place. But with the growth of the population and the increase of intellectuals, the time is coming when America will finally be forced to confront the riddle of homosexuality.[4]

"Men of perverted tendencies"

Analyses of homosexual behavior existed as early as the turn of the century. In this prize-winning essay, published in the *Boston Medical and Surgical Journal* in 1898, a Haverhill, Massachusetts, doctor recommended

that "inverts," in whom homosexuality was innate, should be sent to mental hospitals, while "perverts," who had acquired those tendencies, should be imprisoned:

There is in a community not far removed…men of perverted tendencies, men known to each other as such, bound by ties of secrecy and fear and held together by mutual attraction. This band to whom I refer embraces, not as you might think, the low and vile outcasts of the slums, but men of education and refinement, men gifted in music, in art and in literature, men of business and of affairs. To themselves, by the attraction of their presence and surroundings, they draw boys and young men over whom they have the same jealous bickerings and heart burnings that attend the triumphs of a local belle. Quarrels for preference are frequent, yet must, by the nature of things, be kept to themselves. The triumphant suitor carries to his house and his room the innocent victim, and then begins a course of sexual perversion, the teacher an adept, the pupil a novice, until a new star arises, or satiety compels a rest.[5]

"I was what I was by nature"

In 1924, the cultural historian F. O. Matthiessen, just graduated from Harvard, wrote to his lover, the painter Russell Cheney, about his feelings on reading Carpenter and Ellis:

Yesterday I bought and read through Edward Carpenter's *The Intermediate Sex*. Reading it brought me back to…last spring…[when] I was reading Ellis' volume on inversion. Then for the first time it was completely brought home to me that I was what I was by nature. I sat reading Ellis, sexually aroused, with no hope of ever expressing it…. If I had read this Carpenter book last spring I would have been surprised at the beautiful pictures he gives of love between men. Was it possible for love and friendship to be blended into one?[6]

Matthiessen went on to found the academic discipline known as American studies. He remained with Cheney until the latter's death in 1945. During the McCarthy era, Matthiessen was persecuted for his political views, and he was subjected to a series of investigations into his personal and professional life. He committed suicide in Boston in 1950.

**F. O. Matthiessen and
Russell Cheney**

Passing women

Contemporary records from the first decades of the twentieth century document several instances of "passing women" who dressed, lived, and worked as men. Since men received much higher wages than did women, there was doubtless an economic incentive for many of the women who adopted this lifestyle. (This is in marked contrast to upper-class women, such as the wealthy socialite Eleanora Sears, who were able to cross-dress in public.) Yet posing as male to gain economic advantage does not explain why many of these women chose other women as partners in their emotional and sexual lives.

We will never know how many women passed as men during this period, or how many of their friends, family members, and coworkers knew of their secret. This is because the only known cases of passing women are those who were discovered in the context of a medical emergency, when they ran afoul of the law, or at the time of their deaths.

"HE" WAS A WOMAN

Death in New York of Miss Caroline Hall of Boston.

Registered as a Man on Books of the Steamer Citta di Terino.

Came With a "Wife," Who Was Guiseppina Boriana of Milan— Former Adopted Male Costume Because She Could Get Along Better in the World as a Man Than as a Woman.

From the *Boston Traveler* (1 October 1901)

"Let me die with my secret"

Caroline Hall was the daughter of John Rounsville Hall, a well-known Boston architect. She met her "wife," Giuseppina Boriana of Milan, while living and working as an artist in Europe. This item is from the *Boston Daily Globe,* dated 1 October 1901, which describes Hall's death aboard an Italian steamer en route to visit her dying father:

Caroline Hall…died early yesterday morning on board the Italian steamer *Città di Terino*, which arrived from Naples yesterday afternoon. Until after her death all the 75 passengers on the vessel believed her to be a man.

Accompanied by a woman, "Charles Winslow Hall" boarded the steamer at Naples on Sept. 9. They were entered on the ship's passenger list as husband and wife and occupied a luxurious stateroom on the upper deck. While "Mrs. Hall" found pastime in the ladies' parlor, "Charles Winslow Hall" drank, smoked, and gambled with the men.

The ship's surgeon was summoned to attend "Mr. Hall," who was suffering from consumption, and it was then her true sex was revealed.

With the strength of desperation the woman sprang from her berth and held him fast. She begged and pleaded with him to let her die with her secret. Firmly, but gently, the doctor forced the hysterical woman from him and hastened to inform the captain of his discovery. Aside from these two officers and the woman's companion, not a soul on board the big ship knew what had occurred until the steamer reached quarantine Sunday morning.

While in Naples [Hall] first made the acquaintance of Giuseppina Boriana, a woman of means and culture, and for almost 10 years they have lived and traveled together throughout Europe.

Extensive travel worked a complete revolution in the mind of this remarkable woman. From a happy student of art and history, she developed a violent dislike for those of her own sex. Her admiration for the opposite sex grew into a longing to simulate their habits and dress, and in gratification of this strange desire she affected the garb of a man.

Out on a "lark"

This item, taken from the *Boston Post,* dated 1 July 1920, describes the arrest of two women wearing men's clothing by a police officer:

Two young women garbed in men's clothing were discovered at the corner of Province court and Bromfield street last night by patrolmen. For a time they nearly fooled the officers who had questioned them as to what they were doing there, but a closer inspection revealed the fact that they were of the weaker sex, and they were hustled to the City Hall avenue station.

The women gave their names and said they were out on a "lark." However, the police believe that the names are fictitious. The girls were taken to the House of Detention, where they were told that they would have to stay until they procured women's clothing to wear away.

WOMEN GARBED IN MEN'S SUITS

Lark Lands Couple in Police Station

Headline from the *Boston Post,* 1 July 1920

Notorious woman

Perhaps Boston's most infamous passing woman was Ethel Kimball, a.k.a. James Hathaway. Posing as Hathaway, Kimball married Louise Aechtler in Boston after a two-year courtship. A few months after the wedding, Kimball was arrested on suspicion of car theft, and her true identity was discovered. On 16 December 1921, the *New York Times* printed the following account of the incident, which it described as "one of the strangest cases in the history of the Boston Police Department":

Kimball had been leading a double life for two years, during which she posed as a widower of means...and deceived Louise M. Aechtler, a trusted and respected girl of Somerville, into marrying her.

Not all men with whom the Kimball woman came in contact penetrated her disguise. She posed at various times as the nephew of Richard H. Long, the wealthy Framingham manufacturer, and at another time as the Boston manager of J. Pierpont Morgan's interests. Garbed as a man, she lived opposite the girl she was courting for two years and completely deceived even the girl's relatives. They were married on November 29 by the Rev. Robert Blair at the Union Congregational Church, Columbus Avenue, South End. The now thoroughly disillusioned bride has disappeared....

In her cell [Kimball] talked freely. She had a voice which resembles a man's. Thin-faced, bespectacled, aquiline-nosed, she presented the appearance of the "new woman" artists delighted to depict in male attire in the early days of the suffrage movement.

"I wore men's clothing because I wanted to approach life's problems from a man's viewpoint, especially the problem of unemployment," she said.

Kimball pleaded guilty to falsifying the marriage license. She told the district court that her marriage was a prank and that her "bride" knew she was a woman. One of the greatest difficulties she found in posing as a man, according to Kimball, was in rebuffing flirtatious girls. As reported in the *Boston Globe* on 21 December 1921:

Miss Kimball has devoted her energies to providing for herself a life of gaiety, fine raiment, expensive foods, jewels, automobile rides, and the society of vivacious girls.

COMMONWEALTH OF MASSACHUSETTS

City of Somerville

Certificate of Marriage Intentions

No. 2082

I Hereby Certify, that on the 18th day of November A.D. 1921, the following-named parties caused notice of their intention to be joined in marriage to be entered in this office, and that they have furnished the following facts, which have been duly recorded, viz.:

Name of GROOM, } James William Hathaway,

Residence { 51 Ibbetson Street, Somerville, Mass.

Age. 32 Years,

Occupation, Manufacturer

Place of Birth, Brighton, Boston, Mass.

Name of Father, James W. Hathaway

Maiden Name of Mother, Nathalie Long

Number of the Marriage, first (Widowed or divorced)

Issued at the City Clerk's Office, SOMERVILLE, this

Name of BRIDE. } Louise Marguerite Aechtler

Residence { 55A Lowell Street, Mass., Somerville,

Age. 28 Years,

Occupation, Saleswoman

Place of Birth, Jamaica Plain, Boston, Mass.

Name of Father, Jacob W. Aechtler

Maiden Name of Mother, Babette Raithel

Number of the Marriage, first (Widowed or divorced)

Certif

I Hereby Certify, that I joined the above on the Twenty third day of November Robert Blair (Name) (Residence) 32 Conc

*If other than white, African, Mulatto, Indian or other class

HOLD WOMAN MASQUERADER

Ethel, Alias James, Has Long Police Record

Pleads Not Guilty of Theft, but Seeks No Bail

Wears Regular Woman's Clothing in Court

James A. Hathaway the chaing husband, appeared before Ju e in the Municipal Court yes fternoon and plead charge and

MARRIAGE WAS A PRANK, SHE SAYS

Ethel M. Kimball Appears in Somerville Court

REGISTRY DIVISION, CITY OF BOSTON

COUNTY OF SUFFOLK, COMMONWEALTH OF MASSACHUSETTS, UNITED STATES OF AMERICA

Certificate № 38374 J

CERTIFIED COPY OF RECORD OF **MARRIAGE** IN OFFICE OF THE CITY REGISTRAR

I, the undersigned, hereby certify that I hold the office of .... City Registrar of the City of Boston, and have custody of the Records of Births, Marriages and Deaths required by law to be kept in said City; and I certify that the following facts appear on said Records:

No. 7830 Date of Marriage November 23, 1921 Place of Marriage Boston, Mass

NAME AND SURNAME OF GROOM AND BRIDE	RESIDENCE OF EACH AT TIME OF MARRIAGE	AGE IN YEARS	COLOR	NUMBER OF MARRIAGE (WID. OR DIV.)	OCCUPATION
James W Hathaway	Somerville, Mass	32	White	First	Manufacturer
Louise M Aechtler	Somerville, Mass	28	White	First	Saleswoman

PLACE OF BIRTH OF EACH	NAMES OF PARENTS (MAIDEN NAME OF MOTHER)
Boston, Mass	James W Hathaway - Nathalie Long
Boston, Mass	Jacob W Aechtler - Babette Raithel

NAME, RESIDENCE AND OFFICIAL POSITION OF THE PERSON WHO SOLEMNIZED THE MARRIAGE	DATE OF RECORD
Robert Blair - Clergyman	December 19, 1921
Boston, Mass	--------------------

I further certify that by annexation, the Records of the following-named cities and towns are in the custody of the City Registrar of Boston:—

ANNEXED		ANNEXED	
East Boston	1637	Charlestown	1874
South Boston	1804	Brighton	
Roxbury	1868	West Roxbury	1874
Dorchester	1870	Hyde Park	1912

WITNESS my hand and the SEAL of the CITY REGISTRAR

on this 24th Day of September A.D. 19 79

William J. Kane .... City Registrar

By Chapter 314 of Acts of 1892, "the certificate or attestations of either Assistant City Registrar shall have the same force and effect as that of the City Registrar."

Above, clockwise from top:
Newspaper items pertaining to the Kimball case, which appeared in the *Boston Globe* on 16 and 20 December 1921; certified copy of marriage license between James W. Hathaway and Louise M. Aechtler, 23 November 1921; City of Somerville Certificate of Marriage Intentions, 18 November 1921

Right:
The house in Somerville where Hathaway and Aechtler lived

The early twentieth century: 1900–1945

The *Boston Globe* reported a similar incident in April 1922:

Charlotte Vincent...who yesterday caused a big stir in the Day Square section of Noddle Island by appearing in masculine raiment smoking a cigarette, and "well lit up" with moonshine, was very meek when she was brought before Judge Joseph H. Barnes in East Boston District Court this morning.

Charlotte was not a stranger in the court. She had been there before according to court records, and has served sentences in Lancaster and in the House of the Good Shepherd. In court she had discarded her masculine attire....

The young girl said she did not recall what happened. She admitted that she had been drinking heavily and that her mind was a blank to the things that happened. In view of her record the Judge sent her to Sherborn for an indefinite "vacation."

JAIL GIRL WHO WORE BOY'S SUIT

Miss Charlotte Vincent, 19, of 221 Everett street, East Boston, who was arrested in Day square last night while roistering in men's clothing with a trio of young men, today in East Boston district court pleaded guilty to drunkenness and was given an indefinite sentence to Sherborn.

Patrolman Marnelli attempted to get the boisterous quartet to go home, but the masquerading girl was defiant and refused to obey. She spent the night in a cell.

Article from the *Boston Traveler*, 28 April 1922

Daughter of Fortune

Eleanora Sears, a popular Boston socialite, was a pioneer in women's athletics, and broke ground for other women in previously all-male sports. Her many achievements included being the first national women's squash champion and the first woman to play polo. She was twice National Women's Tennis Doubles champion, and she set numerous records for long-distance walking. In 1912, Sears rode out onto a polo field where a men's team was playing, wearing jodhpurs and sitting astride her horse. She boldly asked to be on the team. Her request was not only denied, but she was told that she was required to ride sidesaddle, and that she should "restrict herself to normal feminine attire in the future." She ignored these requests, and began wearing trousers at all times.[7]

**Opposite:
Eleanora Sears attending a tennis tournament with Miss Isabel Pell in the 1920s**

The early twentieth century: 1900–1945

Right:
This poster advertises a drag ball held in 1914 on "St. Valentine Night" at the Boston Architectural Club. Among the "Principal Lady Characters taking part in our heart-rending melodrama" were "Violette Ophelia" and "Madame Blinkensdorph." The poster describes the highlight of the evening—a wrestling match between the two fair damsels.

"Violette Ophelia will contest also for the Lady Wrestling Championship of Somerset Street against Madame Blinkensdorph. Violette has got to make good against Blinkensdorph or have her salary cut. Madame says Violette is only a phony champ and that she will make her hit the trail for the uncuts. She says she has the champ sized all right this time and will set the pace herself. Last time they wrestled she was nervous and over anxious, but now it will be a different story. Violette says she will throw Madame in 15 minutes or forfeit $10.00 to the Competition Committee."

Boys will be girls

By 1900 minstrel acts had been popular in Boston for a number of years. These acts, many of which featured cross-dressing, centered on portrayals of greatly exaggerated racial and sexual stereotypes. In the first decades of the twentieth century, female impersonators such as Boston natives Julian Eltinge and Neil Burgess achieved national stature. Some of these performers were seen as serious "illusionists" who did not exhibit what is often considered camp behavior. Impersonation was a long-standing tradition, since men had played women's roles on the stage for hundreds of years. This tradition was sustained by male and female undergraduate dramatic societies throughout the Boston area, which often featured cross-dressing in their performances.[8]

Impersonator extraordinaire

Boston-born Neil Burgess achieved fame as one of the greatest impersonators of his day. One account described him as

a big man, without the slightest trace of good looks, [who] could, without difficulty, seem the woman he was playing, whether making a pie in the kitchen, giving a piece of her mind to an interfering interloper, or starting a

young couple on the way to matrimony.[9]

The "ideal woman"

Born and raised in Boston, Julian Eltinge was the most celebrated female impersonator in vaudeville. He began his career with George M. Cohan's touring minstrel shows and eventually amassed a fortune performing as the ideal woman in the United States and Europe. He published his own magazine, in which he often gave advice to women about how to be more beautiful. His personal life was closely scrutinized, and numerous assurances were printed that Eltinge was a "real man" offstage. One such article, which appeared in the *Boston Traveler* on 18 May 1912, was entitled "Eltinge Really a Manly Chap, In Fact His Name is Bill Dalton."

The program from the Boston performance of *Country Fair,* with Neil Burgess starring in the role of Abigail Prue ("prim, prudish, and practical")

The early twentieth century: 1900–1945

"Always wear a bracelet"

These excerpts are taken from an article entitled "How I Make Myself a Beautiful Woman," by Julian Eltinge, which appeared in the *Saturday Evening Traveler* on 12 May 1912, while Eltinge was at the Boston Theatre performing in *The Fascinating Widow*. Eltinge credits Boston girls for inspiration:

In traveling over the country I have come to the conclusion that the Boston girl is the tailor-made type, quite unlike the fluffy ruffle girls I see in other towns, noticeably Baltimore. But when I am speaking of the Boston girls, I do not intend to stop with the maid who lives on Beacon Street, for the girl from South Boston is equally attractive and compares favorably with the heiress in appearance. I have noticed a number of charming Irish-American shop girls since I have been in Boston, and their smartness, in spite of the inexpensive costumes they must wear, makes you take a second glance. If I could go through your large department stores here and make my choice, I could recruit a beautiful chorus from the girls behind the counters in a few minutes. I don't

mind admitting that the feminine role I create, in which I try to make the ideal woman in appearance is a composite picture of two or three Boston girls I knew when I made my home here.

Below is a selection of what the *Traveler* called "Eltingegrams":

•

Powder and rouge the fingers to make them look tapering.

•

Never show the breadth across the back of the hand if you want people to think it is small.

•

Men notice a girl's hands and judge her by them before they notice her face.

•

Always wear a bracelet. It makes the arm look plump.

•

Satin slippers make the feet look smaller than any other kind.

•

Women would improve 50% in appearance if they would take more care of their hair.

•

Red-haired women should wear purple, blue or green, never brown.

•

The secret of smart dressing is contrast in color.

"The Slave of Fashion"

Female impersonator Francis Renault was the featured model in a number of women's fashion shows and burlesque performances. One of his appearances was promoted in the *Boston Traveler* on 23 July 1931:

A special fashion show, sponsored by Francis Renault, "The Slave of Fashion," will be put on at Scollay Square Theatre, tomorrow afternoon. Renault's ability to display the latest and most beautiful feminine creations is well known to Hub theatre-goers, and tomorrow this versatile artist promises many new striking fashion delights.

Opposite:
Francis Renault, "The Slave of Fashion"

Right:
This photo of Renault appeared in the *Boston Herald Traveler* on 5 May 1938 to advertise his appearance in the *White Way Scandals*.

The early twentieth century: 1900–1945

"I had never felt any clear sexual emotion for another man till one spring when we rehearsed and gave…a musical farce for the benefit of our University boat-club.… I had the part of a beautiful princess in this piece.… Soon after the rehearsal in dress came, I began to notice how some of my classmates began to fall in love with me *en scène*. Some even showed the same sentiment afterward."

Anonymous quotation from *The Intersexes,* by Edward Stevenson (1908)

The all-male cast of the
musical *Listening In*, performed by Northeastern
University's Silver
Masque drama club in
1924

ImproperBostonians

Same-sex weddings

These photographs were taken from Simmons College's Freshman-Junior Wedding, which was an annual event from about 1913 through the mid-1940s. The president of the junior class took the part of the groom; the freshman class president was her bride. The marriage ritual was followed to an exacting level of detail—from the stag party to the wedding cake.

The early twentieth century: 1900–1945

Banned in Boston

In the twentieth century, regulation of public behavior was carried out by a number of self-appointed watchdog groups who served as keepers of the city's morals. Backed by laws dating from the eighteenth century, these groups were responsible for what was called by one reporter in 1929 a "dark ages," lasting over thirty-five years, in which more plays and books were forbidden to the populace than at any other time in the city's history. "Banned in Boston" became a phrase known throughout the world. New York producers who didn't send copies of their plays to the city censor to be revised or rewritten faced the possibility of cancellation after the first night. Tickets to the New York run of a performance would often be sent to the censor before the play traveled north, in order for it to be "Bostonized."[10]

One of the city's first censorship groups was the Office of the Clerk's Committee on Theatrical Exhibitions. Representatives from church groups, charitable workers, ladies' aid societies, moral reform societies, and temperance unions met in the late nineteenth century to discuss forming a board of censorship. Speaking in favor of the board, Captain Julius A. Palmer said, "I believe that Boston stands—and I have seen a great deal of the world—at the head of every city in the world in regard to its purity and its morals."[11]

In 1904 the city hired its first chief of the Licensing Division of the Mayor's Office, who served as the city censor, reviewing theatrical performances and literature. (The position existed until the 1980s.) Providing both support and criticism of the city censor were private

THE COMMONWEALTH OF MASSACHUSETTS.

In the year One Thousand Nine Hundred and Fifteen.

AN ACT *Relative to revoking and suspending Licenses for Theatrical and like Exhibitions in the City of Boston.*

Be it enacted by the Senate and House of Representatives in General Court assembled, and by the authority of the same, as follows: SECTION 1. Section one of chapter four hundred and ninety-four of the acts of the year nineteen hundred and eight is hereby amended by adding at the end thereof the words:— The mayor and the police commissioner of Boston and the chief justice of the municipal court of the city of Boston, by a majority vote, may revoke or suspend any such license at their pleasure, — so as to read as follows:— Section 1. The mayor of Boston, except as provided in section forty-six of chapter one hundred and six of the Revised Laws, shall grant a license for theatrical exhibitions, public shows, public amusements and exhibitions of every description, to which admission is obtained upon payment of money or upon the delivery of any valuable thing, or by a ticket or voucher obtained for money or any valuable thing, upon such terms and conditions as he deems reasonable, but there shall not be charged a fee exceeding one hundred dollars for such license when the entertainment, exhibition or show is given in a building licensed as a theatre. A license to be exercised in a building licensed as a theatre shall be for a theatrical season and shall expire on the first day of August of each year. The mayor and the police commissioner of Boston and the chief justice of the municipal court of the city of Boston, by a majority vote, may revoke or suspend such license at their pleasure. SECTION 2. Section two of chapter four hundred and ninety[...] the acts of the year nineteen hundred and eight is hereby repealed. SECTION 3. This act [...] effect upon its passage.

House of Representatives, May [...]

Passed to be enacted, *Channing H. C[...]*

In Senate, [...]

Passed to be enacted, *Calvin Co[...]*

May 21 1915.
Approved,
David I. Walsh

THIRTY-EIGHTH ANNUAL REPORT
OF
The New England
Watch and Ward Society
*Founded in 1878
Incorporated in 1884 in Boston*

FOR THE YEAR 1915-1916

BOSTON:
OFFICE OF THE SOCIETY, 200 EQUITABLE BLDG.
67 MILK STREET
1916

morality groups, such as the New England Watch and Ward Society, the Catholic Church, and another group aligned with the Catholic Church, the League of Decency. These groups were concerned with the issues covered by both the censor and the city's Licensing Board, which granted and revoked liquor licenses based, in part, on the perceived immorality of the staff and patrons.

The Watch and Ward Society, established in 1878 as the New England Society for the Suppression of Vice, investigated crime and moral corruption in the form of gambling, drugs, prostitution, and pornography. Members often attended burlesque shows when traveling out of town, ostensibly so that they could report on how New England's regulations compared to other cities. The society's minutes include the names of virtually all the popular gay bars and gathering places of the time. Bars were frequently under the society's surveillance; its intelligence often contributed to reports to the vice squad and the Licensing Board.[12]

In 1915 Mayor James Michael Curley banned the portrayal of "sex perversion" from music halls and vaudeville stages. As a result, nearly every major theatrical or literary work of the 1920s

and 1930s that dealt even marginally with sexuality was banned in Boston. An ironic exception was *The Well of Loneliness,* Radclyffe Hall's 1928 lesbian novel. When New York censors tried unsuccessfully to ban the novel, a barrage of free publicity ensued that made the book a best-seller. Publisher Donald Friede wrote to the Watch and Ward Society in the hope they would also prosecute. Unfortunately, said Friede, the society "assured me that they saw nothing wrong with the book"—since the lesbian protagonist comes to a miserable end.[13]

Moral watchdogs soon found themselves facing a dilemma: when they banned or censored a work, they risked publicizing the very subject they wished to hide. One example of this occurred in 1935, when Boston Mayor Frederick W. Mansfield gave enormous publicity to Lillian Hellman's *The Children's Hour* by banning it. Mansfield, who admitted he had never seen the play, told the *Boston Traveler* in December 1935 that

[it] showed moral perversion, the unnatural appetite of two women for each other.... There was a place where one person spoke of two women kissing as no woman should kiss another.... [Lesbianism] is an altogether revolting theme and tends

The early twentieth century: 1900–1945

Mary Driscoll, chair of the
Boston Licensing Board

FIGHT BOSTON PLAY BAN.

Author of 'The Children's Hour'
Calls Mayor Arbitrary.'

Lillian Hellman, author of "The
Children's Hour," ...esterday
that she and He...
producer, would...
legally possible'...
tive order of...
Boston bannir...
that city.
"If it is po...
like to make...
arbitrary r...
said.
She and...
see their...
bacher, to...
take any...
order.

to pander to the abnormal appetites of those who are attracted by such stuff.... We can get along without *The Children's Hour.*

Throughout the 1930s and 1940s, the Watch and Ward Society aided the city government in cancelling performances and closing establishments. They reported houses of prostitution to the vice squad, as well as any bars, Turkish baths, businesses, and private homes that they suspected of being homosexual gathering places.[14]

Much of this information was passed along to the notorious Mary Driscoll of the Boston Licensing Board, who was known for her impromptu visits to gay bars in her capacity as guardian of the city's morals. She would remain in the public eye through the 1950s, as the result of her efforts to discourage appearances by the likes of the famous transsexual Christine Jorgensen. Driscoll, who fought to prevent female impersonators from appearing in Boston, was eventually paid the ultimate insult, when drag queens lampooned her in costume at Boston's famous Beaux Arts Ball.[15]

Above, left:
The producers lost the lawsuit mentioned in the clipping, since the play, which had to be shown before it could be banned, never opened in Boston.

Above:
The New York cast of
The Children's Hour

Profile:
Richard Cowan

Richard Cowan was a student at Cornell University in 1932 when he met Stewart Mitchell, an older man who was visiting upstate New York. Mitchell hailed from Boston, where he worked as editor of the *Dial,* a literary magazine. When Cowan moved to Cambridge after graduation to work as a landscape architect, Mitchell set him up in an apartment.

Cowan's diary, begun at Cornell, details his life as a gay man. Like many homosexuals of the time, Cowan had difficulty managing his personal affairs. He committed suicide in Gloucester in 1938. The diary begins in 1933.

[I was in a] despondent state of mind and went so far as to cry on Eliz. shoulder one night. I thought a lot about suicide but then there was Mother to think of. I have no fear of death and think if I could take gas or some such thing I'd be ready to die now. Were it not for hurting Mother and Stewart, I would. Wrote a long and depressing letter to Stewart, who replied that I should come to Boston & stay as long as I liked. He sent a check for carfare and here I am.

For the first few weeks I went through Hell! Mrs. T., Stewart, and Pinkie were the only persons I knew in Boston, and I saw very little of them. It was a great jump from the many acquaintances of Ithaca to solitude in a strange city. It was not until last June that Stewart and I had any physical relations. I walked the streets nights and allowed myself to be picked up. Met a Dartmouth boy on the Common one night after the Symphony. Made a date with him for the next day but as I gave him the wrong telephone number (unintentionally) I didn't see him again till after Xmas when I met him at the Symphony. His name was Jack and he lived with his family in Newton.

Some time before Thanksgiving I started going to the hotel at 5 every evening. Stewart & I would walk for an hour or so. Then dine with Mrs. T., and I'd talk to her and play the victrola 'till about eleven while Stewart worked on his thesis. They were very pleasant evenings and I think we all enjoyed them. Mother came on a week or so before Thanksgiving and stayed for two weeks with me in Plympton street.

Took her to theatres, etc. & saw all the sights of Boston. She enjoyed it very much and hated to go home. She liked both Stewart & Mrs. T.—but I wonder just what she thinks & how much she knows of Stewart & me. I went home for two weeks at Christmas but was glad to return to Cambridge.

Soon after returning I saw Jack in the Symph[ony] Hall and saw a good bit of him thereafter. He was a bit obvious but I liked him. He claimed he loved me etc. Stayed at his home one Saturday night while visiting some friends of his I met George, a Dartmouth boy living in Wellesley Hills. He called me the next day & I went to the movies, with him—and that started that. I think I really did love him at first and he—very passionately—said he loved me. Stayed with me in Plympton Street quite often and we walked with Stewart one evening. S. didn't like him and I'm sure was very jealous. I love S. very much but am incapable of being true to anyone person. Eventually George's phone calls, letters, and jealous scenes became unbearable.

Finally not having seen him for some time, he came to see me and demanded his letters back. Sayed [sic] that I should explain, etc. I told him I had nothing to explain and since he had proposed it, I thought it best not

to see one another again. That led to a theatrical scene—in which G. felt quite at home. He begged me to take him back but I refused. It went on for some time till finally I asked him to leave and went into the bathroom. Then, in came G. with his mouth stained with iodine and bade me a tearful adieu. That cured any love I still had for him! I called him a fool— and made him drink half a glass of castor oil & orange juice. I didn't tell him what it was and I hope it cured him. Told him he might call me in a week. He called before that and I saw him a couple of times, and then ignored him. Had a note on my birthday asking me to see him before he left in Oct. Don't know where he's going or whether he is going away but am ignoring the note. I think his love is more self-pity & cheap theatricals than true affection. George was an intimate friend of Abram Piatt Andrew, congressman from Gloucester [see pages 90 and 92]. Andrew, it seems, is about a fifth cousin of Stewart, and since his home is in Gloucester, both Stewart & Mrs. Thomas knew him. Late in the spring he stayed at the Statler one night and George asked me there to meet him. We had lots of gin and all got drunk. Both of them wanted me to stay all night but I refused. Also went to the Ritz one night to meet another friend of George, Ben, just back from Paris for a few days. Both were old men—too old for me.

One night, at the Monarch Club, I met a boy whom I had seen before at the Copley Theatre & once in the subway—Ned, a singer. I was very drunk and foolishly told him I loved him. Common sense would have told him that I didn't know what I was talking about. Saw him several times and slept with him in Plympton street. He's in Gloucester this summer working & singing in the Blacksmith Shop in Rockport. See him every now & then.

Came to Gloucester to stay with S. & Mrs. T. on the 14th of May. The next week I went to Boston & had my tonsils out at the Phillips House where I stayed for five days.

Returned to Gloucester for several days and then—since another of Mrs. T.'s protégés was coming to visit her—I went home for a couple of weeks. Stayed at the hotel for a couple of nights. While there I went to see Catherine Cornell in *Alien Corn*. Well played but depressing. In the lobby a boy & I eyed one another. After the show he followed me up the street and we went to the Public Garden & talked. His name is Ray from Stoneham. I told him I was staying at

the Somerset and he left to catch the midnight train. When I returned to the hotel he called me & said he'd missed his train. Result—we went to P. St. & slept together. He's a fine kid but melancholy & has the falling-in-love-with-me-sickness. He's working in Sea-Bright, N.Y. this summer & has sent letter after letter. Will see him this fall but must make it clear that I'm not interested.[16]

Richard Cowan in his ROTC uniform at Cornell, c. 1930

126 **Private snapshot of two
sailors camping it up in
the Back Bay, c. 1944**

"I didn't know the word *homosexual* until I was in the john while living in the barracks in Germany. I guess there were two guys there and they didn't realize anybody else was in there. They were talking, and I realized, 'My God, what they're talking about is what I feel!' That was the first time I heard the word *homosexual*."

—Anonymous quotation

128   Goodenough Test drawings by men in the "feminine" group (above) and the "masculine" group (below). The men whose drawings placed them in the "feminine" group were detained for further tests to determine their masculinity. Army regulations strictly forbade the drafting of homosexuals.

Life during wartime

World War II uprooted men and women across the country, often placing them in same-sex environments for the first time. The proximity of Boston to nearby naval bases resulted in an influx of servicemen during the war that greatly expanded Boston's gay subculture and provided men with numerous opportunities for comradeship and casual sex. Life during wartime also created opportunities for women who chose to work and live a single life away from the watchful eyes of their families. Lesbians in suburban or rural areas who came to Boston found both jobs and a greater degree of sexual freedom. For both sexes, the thrill of relationships and encounters was both mitigated and intensified by the threat of discovery and the peril of living in a world at war.

The Goodenough Test

Men signing up for the military often were given tests like the Goodenough Drawing a Man Test, which was designed to detect "inner homosexual tendencies" from the appearance of "feminine characteristics"—large eyes with lashes, a curved figure, or graceful posture—in the drawing of male figures. In 1943 and 1944, the military also used a "blue discharge"—regularly

World War II Coast Guardsman

given to social misfits of all stripes, from addicts to psychopaths—to remove thousands of gay soldiers without courts-martial. Immediately after the war, the blue discharge was dropped, and homosexuals not guilty of any definite offenses would receive a dishonorable discharge.[17]

The Buddies Club

The [Lighthouse] bar was on the second floor. It was always filled with sailors during the war. People didn't have time to think about right or wrong. The war was going on. If you'd see somebody today you might never see them again tomorrow. People met. They didn't have time to think about whether they should do something. They were here now and just enjoyed life today because they might be dead tomorrow.[18]
—Conrad S.

Places to meet

Scollay Square, Boston's entertainment district until the early 1960s, was home to a number of bars, such as the Crawford House, frequented by gay men and lesbians. Many gay men went to these bars in the hope of meeting sailors, who themselves had gone to see female strippers, such as Sally Keith and "Peaches, Queen of the Shakes." One gay man described the atmosphere at the Lighthouse, another Scollay Square establishment, as follows:

A home away from home

During World War II, the Buddies Club opened on the Boston Common, a location already well known to gay men for anonymous nocturnal encounters. The club remained on the site until the mid-1960s, when it was replaced by a tourist information booth:

It was built for the servicemen during the war—a place where they could go and play cards, or go and read and have something to eat. It was a home away from home. I'm sure they met men there.
—Conrad S.

Half Dollar   Lighthouse   Crawford House

Scollay Square, Boston's entertainment district until the early 1960s, was home to a number of bars frequented by gay men and lesbians. Three of those establishments are visible in this 1940s photo.

The early twentieth century: 1900–1945

Breaking away

The defense industry and the civilian workplace afforded lesbians the chance to break away from their families—or at least to avoid expectations of marriage and children. The influx of women into previously all-male workplaces, the military, and the civilian defense corps offered a sense of independence and self-confidence, while providing opportunities for lesbian relationships to develop. Some reminiscences follow:

[In 1943] I joined the WAC, which was an auxiliary corps to the Army. I trained in Massachusetts at Fort Devens and was ultimately assigned to the Boston Army base. I was eventually sent to the Franklin Square House in the South End of Boston on West Newton Street. It was called a home hotel for women and was rather proper in its day. There were a lot of older women living there at the time, but the corps took over the two top floors. My commanding officer turned every head at the Boston Army base—5'6", curly blonde hair, cute as can be and a smart cookie. She played around, but she had a partner in Georgia.
—Jean S.

In this passage, Jean describes how patriotism overshadowed lesbian feelings among women who participated in the war effort:

There were a lot of service people in Boston. It was very casual—always in the face of tragedy we all banded together. Service people were invited everywhere. We were entertained. We were all one.

[I joined the WACs without] any thought in mind of cruising over the whole detachment. [It] was strictly a feeling of patriotism at the time. I think we all felt that way. Never giving lesbianism a second thought other than being very covert about it. Always extremely careful. Always brushed under the carpet.

There was a bar three blocks away called Bernstein's where we'd all hang out. There were women in the detachment who I knew were lesbians, there was no question in my mind, but we never spoke of this. You just didn't at that time. You just wouldn't make any reference to it. We would socialize together, both straight and lesbian.[19]

This group of photographs of WACs during World War II (pages 133–135) were taken at the Boston army base and at Franklin Square House.

One of the photographers, who also appears in the photos, was employed by the Army Signal Corps.

"She never spoke to me again"

Living and working together in close quarters and often separated from their men, many women entered into intense friendships that often had strong sexual overtones. One woman describes two such instances of unrequited romance.

There weren't too many men around, and those who were around were either old and crippled or not very satisfactory in one way or another. At the time I was very naive. I had not had a relationship with anyone, and I knew what my feelings were, but I hadn't really expressed them. A woman I worked with suggested one night that we go to the movies. She said, "You know it's going to be late when we get home, so why don't you stay over with me." So we went to the movies and we went back to her place, and we went to bed, and we got into her double bed, and she started to cuddle up and I turned over and went to sleep, and she never spoke to me again.

I had another great friend whose husband was in the service. We did everything together except go to bed together. I realized afterward that she was missing her husband. She would always have me over to her apartment. She would go around to the butcher, this was during meat rationing, and she would say, "You know, I have a serviceman coming home and I need some meat." Finally he said to her, "You know an awful lot of servicemen who are returning." She had me to dinner and we'd sit on the floor and listen to music and we'd sit close together. I thought it was great, but there was no physical attraction. This went on for quite some time until her husband came home and she called and said, "I don't need to see you anymore." I was shocked because we had such a good time together. I guess she was expecting something more to happen, and nothing did.[20]
—Louise Y.

The early twentieth century: 1900–1945

David Walsh

David Ignatius Walsh (1872–1947), the ninth of ten children in an Irish immigrant family, worked his way through high school, graduated from College of the Holy Cross and Boston University Law School, and served two terms as Massachusetts governor before being elected to the U.S. Senate in 1918. As governor, he signed the act of 1915, which permitted censorship of various public entertainments. He supported women's suffrage, workers' safety, and Roosevelt's New Deal. Before the bombing of Pearl Harbor, he had opposed U.S. entry into World War II. Subsequently he became a staunch supporter of the war effort and was appointed chairman of the Senate Naval Committee. Walsh never married. He lived with four of his unmarried sisters and a male Filipino servant who, for thirty years, was his closest companion.

In 1942 authorities raided a house in Brooklyn, New York, where well-to-do civilians gathered to meet sailors from the nearby Brooklyn Navy Yard, as well as other young military men. (Composer Virgil Thomson was arrested in the same raid.) Suspicious of the constant comings and goings to and from the house, neighbors had called the police, who contacted the Bureau of Navy Intelligence. The soldiers and sailors were drinking with the clients and possibly having illegal sex with them. To make matters worse, some of the clients were Germans whom the bureau suspected of being Nazi spies.

Walsh's presence at the house became public when Gustave Beekman, its owner, decided to name names after the judge in the case threatened him with a harsh sentence for operating an establishment where enemy agents had obtained information. Beekman identified one of the regulars, Doc, as Senator Walsh. Walsh denied that he was Doc, although he was also identified by other clients. He had not been observed by the federal agents who staked out Beekman's house but, as head of the naval committee, he may have been tipped off to the raid.

The *New York Post* broke the story, claiming that the dignitary previously identified as "Senator X" was Walsh. His fellow senators were outraged. According to the *New York Times,* a group of senators called for an investigation to determine whether there was a conspiracy to smear members of Congress who had opposed U.S. entry into the war. Senate Majority Leader (later Vice President) Alben Barkley announced that J. Edgar Hoover, director of the FBI, had cleared Walsh of the charge of visiting with enemy aliens in Beekman's house. Walsh denounced the charge to Barkley as a "diabolical lie" and recovered his reputation.[21]

In an interview conducted for Boston's *Fag Rag* in 1974, the writer Gore Vidal observed, "There wasn't anybody in Massachusetts from the little birds on the Common who didn't know what David Walsh was up to." Vidal claimed Walsh had tried to "make" his father, Eugene Vidal, when the elder Vidal was a West Point cadet. Vidal remembered that his father "went absolutely to pieces" when, as director of the Bureau of Air Commerce in the Roosevelt administration, he was asked to testify before a Senate committee. "I always told him that way in the back of his mind there was the memory of his bad experience of Senator Walsh. So he regarded all senators as potential rapists and pederasts."[22]

The following limerick was written in 1947 to commemorate the raid on the Beekman house:

Said Senator David I. Walsh,
"These charges against me are falsh.
*   Though I did go to Brooklyn*
*   For sooklyn and fooklyn,*
Not a gob laid his hands on my balsh."[23]

The early twentieth century: 1900–1945

The men of the *Baltimore*

The following pages present a rare glimpse into gay social life. Boston resident Preston Claridge's reminiscences from just after World War II describe a number of get-togethers between gay men and servicemen. Several of these encounters involved Claridge's friends and the marines assigned to a navy ship, the *Baltimore:*

One of my friends gave a party for all the Marines on the *Baltimore* at the Copley Plaza. They weren't at all ashamed of their relationships with gay men because they all came together to this party—15 or 20 of them were all there.... Forty-odd years ago homosexuality was not so well known and so they hadn't learned that you shouldn't associate with homosexuals. [My friend] loved servicemen. He had met a number of the *Baltimore* Marines and so I guess he suggested to one, "Why don't I give a party for all of you." So they said, "Sure." There were no women, which didn't bother the Marines.

The *Baltimore* was a ship with a contingent of about 40 Marines, and I think among us—myself and friends—[we] must have had about 90% of those Marines on the *Baltimore*. Once they discovered they could get a little cash and free food and so forth and a good time with gay people, they

seemed to fall all over themselves to meet us and go with us. They weren't the least bit embarrassed.... Of course, most of them were straight.[24]

Veronica the sailor

Claridge also chronicles a "tea party" held in Wellesley in the mid-1940s, at the home of a professor who had his own darkroom:

One Sunday [Freddie] took me along to a "new faces" party given by Bernard.... Since the beginning of the war, several years before, Bernard had been having "tea dances" for his gay friends and servicemen. Tea was never served, but the scotch flowed and dancing did follow. It was there I danced with a beautiful blonde sailor nicknamed Veronica because of his Veronica Lake style hair falling over one eye. I thought his hair terribly long and feminine at the time but it couldn't have been since he was in the service.

Above, left, and
pages 140–141:
A "tea party" in Wellesley

The early twentieth century: 1900–1945

Opposite:
Veronica (left), fox-
trotting with a pilot

Left:
Veronica (right) and a
soldier in an embrace

Below:
Veronica the morning
after

The early twentieth century: 1900–1945

From the Cold War to Stonewall: 1945–1969

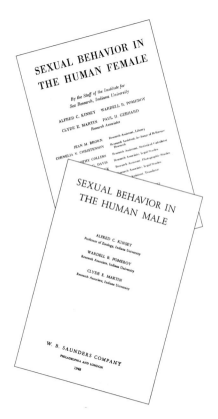

The evolution of Boston's lesbian and gay communities from the end of World War II until the Stonewall rebellion is characterized by steady progress in the face of often intense oppression. The publication of the Kinsey reports on male and female sexuality in 1948 and 1953 rocked the nation, due in large part to the statistics they reported regarding surprisingly high levels of homosexual behavior among individuals of both sexes. After the sacrifices of the Depression and the war, many Americans were encouraged to reclaim rigid, conventional notions of sexual roles, including those pertaining to same-sex relationships. Heightened concerns regarding national security helped to provoke the Cold War and the hysteria of the McCarthy era; many homosexuals were targeted in the ensuing witch hunts of the period.

Boston's gay communities continued to coalesce despite constant threats of blackmail, exposure, public censure, and imprisonment. These trends, which are chronicled in the final section of *Improper Bostonians,* took a number of forms. Years before the gay press emerged, Boston's *Mid-Town Journal* provided a wealth of anecdotal infor-

mation regarding the activities of Boston's lesbians, gays, bisexuals, and transgendered people in the years following World War II. During the 1950s, Boston blueblood Prescott Townsend spearheaded some of the first efforts to organize homosexuals as a political constituency. A distinct bar culture was also emerging in Boston, comprising lively meeting places and equally colorful personalities.

Growing out of the political and social activism of the 1960s, gay liberation emerged at the end of the decade—a movement symbolically linked with New York's Stonewall riots of June 1969. From that moment on, Boston's lesbian and gay community began to assert itself as a viable, visible, and increasingly vocal presence in the city's political and cultural life.

This "Homo Questionnaire'" found in the papers of a Boston social worker, was developed for use by Selective Service agents in the early 1950s to ferret out homosexuals registering for military service. Agents were instructed to look for "flashy jewelry" and "rouge, lipstick, [or] eyebrow pencil." Questions asked included, "How many in your family practice sexual perversion?" and "Ever perform the homo act before an audience?"

Selectee is Masculine - Feminine. Voice is: husky, soft, effiminate (cross ou

Dress is: Flashy, Conservative. Zoot,

Appeared nervous, composed, reluctant to talk (cross out)

Uses Make up: Rouge, Lipstick, Power, Eyebrow pencil (cross out)

Feminine or Masculine gestures. Any flashy jewlery

Remarks

HOMO QUESTIONNARE

1. Age_____ Race_____ Color_____ Nationality_____ Education_____

How Often_____

Wages_____ Use Narcotics_____

2. Employed as_____ Started Homo relations at age of_____

3. Arrested For_____ Age of other person_____ Where_____

4. With whom_____ Did You like it_____

Any heterosexual relations_____

General Impression of Female Sex_____

Orgasim?_____

7. Any Sodomy_____ How often_____ Do you like it_____

How many in your family practice sexual

8. Are you active or passive_____ perversion_____

Does your family know of your condition_____

How often do you practice homosexuality_____ How much_____

Do you ever pay for it_____ Get paid_____

Any special friends_____ Do you consider yourself married_____

When was your last act_____

Ever attend drags_____ Do you like them_____

Do you impersonate women_____

Ever perform the homo act before an audience_____ Under what circumstances_____

Use Make Up_____ Wear Feminine underwear_____

Ever watch two bulldikers perform_____

Any Venereal Diseases_____

What reaction if any_____ Do you allow yourself to be picked up_____

How long were you treated_____

Do you pick people up_____ Where_____ Mutual?_____

Do you masturbate_____ How frequently_____ Do you feel that you

What type of individual do you prefer_____ are normal_____ Did you ever seek advice about your problem_____

Are you happy_____

Do you think you will ever change or get married_____

What do you think is responsible for your condition_____

(Answer on reverse side under "Remarks")

The Cold War

During the years following World War II, fears about the nation's security reached a level of near hysteria. For lesbians and gay men, one of the most devastating manifestations of this chilling trend was an escalation in the number of dishonorable military discharges granted to homosexuals, which increased from slightly over a thousand per year in the late 1940s to more than three thousand annually by the early 1960s.[1]

Because lesbians and gay men were considered part of this subversive threat, they became the targets of political witch hunts that spread to civilian jobs. A Senate subcommittee concluded in 1950:

It is the opinion of this subcommittee that those who engage in acts of homosexuality and other perverted sex activities are unsuitable for employment in the Federal government. The lack of emotional stability which is found in most sex perverts and the weakness of their moral fiber makes them susceptible to the blandishments of foreign espionage agents.[2]

Publicity given to the firings of thousands of government workers and the blacklisting of Hollywood writers and actors created a fearful atmosphere in most gay communities. Yet in marshaling the resources of the state and the media against homosexuals, the McCarthy-era campaigns unwittingly helped weld those subcultures together. The penalties directed at gay men and lesbians grew so intense that they fostered a collective consciousness of oppression that would continue to build momentum during the 1950s and 1960s.

"Nobody dared to breathe"

This firsthand account comes from a woman who was the subject of an FBI investigation:

During the McCarthy era we were doing some work for the government at a local university...so we had to be cleared by the FBI. We were on pins and needles until we finally got the OK. If they had ever found out that we were lesbians we never would have been accepted.... This was right in the middle of the purge in Washington. It was somewhere in the early '50s.... Nobody dared to breathe. It was a pretty scary time. I remember getting a call from an old boss who said, "You know, the FBI was in here today asking questions about you." They wouldn't tell him why.[3]
—Louise Y.

Profile:
Miriam Van Waters

In 1948 a three-hundred-page report ordered by the commissioner of the Massachusetts Department of Corrections detailed charges of immorality at the Women's Reformatory at Framingham. The report targeted Miriam Van Waters, a longtime social reformer, who served as superintendent of the reformatory from 1932 to 1957. Her accusers, angered at her indenture program for inmates, demanded that she treat the reformatory as a prison. The Boston papers also reported incidents of "shocking sex perversion" at the reformatory. Van Waters was suspended when the scandal broke.

When the charges of permissiveness regarding lesbianism at Framingham were made public, an undercurrent of rumors about Van Waters led her to destroy her personal correspondence with her lifelong friend and companion of twenty-two years. Women from all walks of life rallied to her side during the hearings at Boston's State House. On 18 November 1948, the *Boston Traveler* reported the reaction of the audience who packed the chambers:

Front page from the
Boston Traveler,
13 September 1948

From the Cold War to Stonewall: 1945–1969

Benches, aisles and the back of the hearing room were jammed with spectators, most of them women, whose partisanship for Dr. Van Waters became eloquent when they applauded the end of her initial statement at such length and with such vehemence that Chairman J. Elmer Callahan of the commission threatened to stop the hearing.

The commissioner's determination to dismiss Van Waters forced her to seek appeal in another public hearing. Support for Van Waters remained overwhelming, with letters coming from Boston women's groups, professional social work organizations, her friend Eleanor Roosevelt, and even the Watch and Ward Society. Van Waters returned to work at Framingham while the charges and investigations continued. She retired in 1957.[4]

Top left:
Van Waters and her attorneys at her State House hearing

Top right:
Spectators at Van Waters's State House hearing

Bottom:
Miriam Van Waters returning to the Women's Reformatory after her reinstatement in 1949

"What makes a girl turn queer?"

Even after Van Waters left Framingham, lesbianism remained an issue. In
a lecture series held there in 1959,
cosponsored by the Massachusetts
Correctional Institute and the Massachusetts Society for Social Hygiene, a
female psychiatrist answered the questions of twenty-five young prisoners on
the topic of sex. Of the ten questions
asked by the prisoners, seven dealt
with lesbianism.

I will begin with the first question:
"What makes a girl turn queer?" This
is a good question, because the girl
knows or senses that girls are not born
queer, they turn queer....

Society as a whole is quite violently
opposed to homosexuality. [It] can
never be accepted by the world at
large. If all people were to become
homosexuals there would be no further reproduction. The world would
end more slowly but just as surely as
by the atom bomb.

She goes on to deliver her analysis of
lesbian behavior to the prisoners:

There are two kinds of Lesbians: the
"studs," who in medical terms are
called active Lesbians, and the
"Queens" or "Dolls" who are passive
Lesbians. The stud goes on real campaigns to make other girls go to bed
with her. The method is really quite
simple. She feels like a man, she acts
like a man or boy, prefers wearing
slacks or levis, walks like a man, cuts
her hair very short. Her ambition is to
make other girls feel that she is a man.
She becomes quite an expert in knowing how to make love—will kiss a girl
on the lips, first fleetingly and, if the
girl responds, then in more soulful
fashion.

Although she would like to be a
man, her body build is that of a
woman; and so she very well knows
which parts of a girl's body to touch to
make that girl get excited. Because she
knows exactly how a girl feels she may
be expert in all forms of preliminary
excitement of her partner; but because
she does not possess a male organ, it
is doubtful whether she can ever bring
a girl to the same kind of climax that a
man can.[5]

The *Mid-Town Journal*

During the years between 1938 and 1966, finding clues about activities in Boston's homosexual subculture was as easy as picking up a copy of the *Mid-Town Journal,* which was widely distributed throughout Greater Boston. Its editor, Frederick Shibley, was a former acrobatic dancer and burlesque performer, whose noms de plume included Iben Snupin and Cassandra de Swisch. Shibley described the paper as a chronicle of

the unbelievable panorama of life in one of the most fantastic sections of the United States—the South End of Boston. Against a backdrop of exclusive Union Park, mysterious Chinatown, the dingy Bay Village section, and a whirling Sepia Belt, transpires all of the bizarre activity presented in the pages. Bazos, prostitutes, pimps, wife-beaters, stumble-bums, murderers, moochers, homo-sexuals, scavengers and a generous assortment of charlatans exist (rather precariously) in the South End, which is one of the largest rooming house sections in the world.[6]

Shibley's extraordinary chronicle of life in the South End and elsewhere was heavily colored by his singular style, philosophy, and preoccupations. Possessed of his own criminal record, he was fascinated with the daily dramas unfolding in Boston's courtrooms. In publishing the *Journal,* he sought to uncover the humorous side of these stories. A regular attendee at municipal court sessions, he also encouraged his network of friends, neighbors, and law enforcement officials to bring him their juiciest gossip. As a result, the *Journal's* pages were overflowing with tales of marital discord, cohabitation, assault, shoplifting, and the like. Many of these articles focused on the activities of lesbians and gay men, who often ran afoul of the law for transgressions such as soliciting, kissing in public, dressing in drag, and other "lewd and lascivious" behaviors.

In recounting the misadventures of improper Bostonians, Shibley (who was heterosexual) unwittingly created a comprehensive, day-by-day account of the city's lesbian and gay community during a period when gays were virtually invisible in the media. While his convoluted prose is rife with racial and sexual stereotypes, Shibley's commitment to preserving the content of ordinary lives, and his rage against the hypocrisy of social institutions, resulted in an extraordinary chronicle of gay life during the years before gay liberation.[7]

An admirer of the *Journal* sent this poem to the editor in 1949 expressing his delight and amazement at finding such a chronicle of gay life:

To Cassandra de Swisch

In dialect extraordinary
You tell the doom of some poor fairy,
And when the Cossacks feel a yen
To go and bag some twilight man,
You tell us of the whole affair
In double-talk that makes us stare.

'Til recently we never knew
A scribe existed such as you,
In subtlety without compare,
In all the haunts of Copley Square,
Your stories are our favorite disch,
O mister (Missus, Miss) de Swisch!

—signed Faithful Reader

Shibley delighted in elaborate headlines, composed in grand tabloid style, and sentences that could run on for entire paragraphs. The following item appeared in 1960:

Lynn Youth's Special Trip to Hub To Beat Lavender Men Ends In Clink After Park Square Jam

A youth who formed a posse in Lynn and descended on the Park Square area to harass some of the odd cult individuals referred to as lavender men, queers, fags, twilight men, homos and various other less euphemistic terms, was let off with a three-month suspended sentence in Central court, following an unprovoked attack on a soprano-voiced male.

Surprised not too long ago when he first learned that nonconformists existed, and amazed when someone told him of their activities, Dennis T. found it hard to believe.... Had he searched closely enough he would have unquestionably found dozens of them in his own home town of Lynn and some might be executives, auto mechanics, waiters, or even wrestlers but he might not recognize them as they might not have their lashes beaded, brows plucked or tresses curled.

"Sin Chariots" on Summer Street

Articles in the *Journal* often contained a degree of homosexual innuendo not normally associated with the tolerance levels of the postwar era. In the following item, dated 23 September 1949, a "gob" (sailor) is discovered with another man, who was known by the sobriquet Drop-Flap Annie. According to the *Journal,* Annie's car, which was parked outside the barracks, was decorated with venetian blinds and upholstery featuring "large red poinsettias embroidered on a gay background of 'subdued' chartreuse." The *Journal* article follows:

Sex-Buggy Drivers Held, Dicks In Hunt For Gobs Of Love

Cruising along the Summer St. bridge in highly perfumed "Sin Chariots" and luring unsuspecting sailors into strangely-equipped cars with displays of whiskey bottles and some "French pictures," two Hub twilight men were the first captives in the bring-'em-back-alive crusade that was launched by the United States Navy and the Police Department, to round up persistent homosexuals who prey upon and constantly annoy the lonely sailors stationed at the Fargo Building in South Boston. One Boston belle, affectionately known as "Drop Flap

Annie," was trapped in his car parked in a vacant lot on D St., just as a gob was about to guzzle his hootch and he was bent over the dashboard trying to dial in the program: "Can You Top This?"

The judge sent Annie to Deer Island for six months and revoked his driver's license, ruling that improper persons should not operate a motor vehicle.

Nickel droppers

The public toilets located throughout Boston's subway system served as meeting places for "Subway Sammies" until they were closed in the mid-1960s and early 1970s. A "nickel dropper" would enter the rest room and place a nickel on a shelf by the door. The nickel would alert the next arrival that a willing sexual partner was waiting. In 1951 the *Journal* reported on this elaborate system for arranging sexual encounters, and the equally elaborate system used to monitor them:

Sammies Sprout from Subway to Elevated Antics

Reports from uninitiated suburbanites who made temporary stops in the men's lounge in the Egleston Elevated station to police of Division 9, that peculiar characters were using the emergency room for a combination reception hall and love nest, resulted in the assignment of officers to keep the room under surveillance, and brought about the arrest of two men who introduced themselves to each other through a 2-inch hole between the partitions drilled there specifically, it is believed, for that purpose.... Their subsequent convictions in court [followed] testimony by the officers, who observed the activities of the couple through a secret panel recently installed by the M.T.A. to capture perverts that even Dr. Kinsey in moments of his wildest imagination might have difficulty in visualizing.

Detectives who were assigned to the Rest Room Regiment...stated they had been in their secret compartment adjoining the rest room for nearly 50 minutes taking turns peeking when a man entered the rest room, deposited his nickel in the customary place and vanished. A few minutes later another man entered and he too vanished after spending a nickel. The officers, who were located in a position where they could observe both, told the court that they first saw Lloyd peek through the hole in the partition, and when Daniel saw an eye revolving in the hole he decided to look too. He peeked and that was when their eyes first met and it was a case of love at first sight.

Following their novel meeting, Lloyd dropped in for a visit with Daniel and while they were chatting about Paris the officers dropped in and arrested both.

"She was a he"

Over the years, the *Journal* chronicled a number of instances of men attempting to pass as women, and vice versa. Stories such as these provide rare glimpses into the lives of transgendered individuals during the postwar years. One 1946 item describes a sixteen-year-old who

went basso before the horrified eyes of his employer, a respectable woman who had engaged him as a maid.... She notified police, who conducted an investigation and arrived at the conclusion that she was a he.

Another item, published in 1949, describes a homeless "shemale" who had been taken into custody on vagrancy charges:

The refusal of the woman to discard her brown leather jacket, dungarees and paratrooper's boots led to questioning, and the gleaning of information that she was slowly but surely turning into a man.

From the Cold War to Stonewall: 1945–1969

"Cavorting of the two females"

Shibley's descriptions of lesbian antics were equally vivid, as this 1961 item illustrates:

Bar Bussing Bags Babes: Kissing Cuties' Cafe Cavorting Snags Butch, Doll

Puckering her lips and throwing her head back when an attractive blonde clad in a pair of tight fitting slacks put her arms around her, a tiny but beautiful hundred-pound brunette who accepted a hackle-raising kiss as her attractive companion ran her hands over her body, lingering at intimate parts of her anatomy as they squirmed dissolutely, was the picture painted in Central Court by a headquarters detective, who interrupted the cavorting of the two females in a Washington Street cafe, and placed both under arrest on charges of being lewd persons.

Detective Condon of police headquarters, who was on a routine check of the various cafes in the City, relating the incident in Central Court that landed blonde but mannishly attired Beatrice along with beautiful dark tressed Irene in the clink, testified that with detective Murphy he visited the cafe on 90 Washington Street on a routine check. While there he saw Beatrice dancing with Irene and when they returned to their table he saw Beatrice put her arms around Irene and kiss her on the lips. Then he saw Beatrice, who stated she is married, run her hands over Irene's body, stopping at various vital parts and snuggling close to her.

The detective placed both under arrest, he informed the court. At police headquarters, where he questioned both of the girls, Irene stated that the only reason she went there was because, "All of the gay kids were there."

Beatrice, who appeared in court wearing a leather jacket, denied that she kissed Irene and insisted that all she did was talk to her and put her hand on her shoulder. During his testimony the detective disclosed that Irene always dressed properly. But Beatrice, who had a boyish haircut, was usually attired in dungarees or toreador trousers, as many of the females who patronize the cafe are.

The court ordered a guilty verdict and probationed both girls, with the warnings to dress properly to Beatrice, and advised Irene to conduct herself as a female, and not a lollipop for the native butches.

"A wake of perfume"

Although he documented the lives of individuals on the fringes of Boston society, Shibley often resorted to racial and gender stereotypes, as this 1965 piece about an African American transvestite illustrates:

Flat Footed, Congo Curled, Cocoa Cutie, Flop As American Beauty

Spotted by police as she paddled along Columbus avenue in the wee hours of morn wriggling her ample hips provocatively and flashing her white tusks at passing autoists as even the dual headlights took their eyes off the road for a scant fraction of a second in an attempt to identify the odd creature with the oversized feet, the hefty shoulders and thick neck, a Roxbury meanderer who tossed an extra flip of the toga for those who might be interested in striking up an acquaintance, landed in the pokey when a member of the vice squad who recognized the offender stepped out of a vehicle, said "You again," before whisking it off to a cell.

After spending a few hours at Police Headquarters, the offender was transferred to the City Prison....

As he was led to his cell along one of the many tiers, the offender left a wake of perfume that drew whistles and whoopees from some of the boys awaiting trial for more respectable crimes such as robbery, burglary, shootings and stabbings....

In Central Court, where he appeared in the men's side of the dock, the presiding jurist looked up and asked the court officer, "Why is she in the men's dock?" and an officer from the morality squad who heard the question answered, "Your honor, she's a he. That is, a man!"

The prisoner grinned and tossed his bongo curls and his still creamed face glistened as he pleaded not guilty to idle and disorderly conduct charges.

The court couldn't send him to the World's Fair to represent Boston, as the Fair hasn't opened yet. The Women's Reformatory was out, as no males are allowed. At Deer Island, someone might drown him, so Lady Talbot was ordered to serve 20 days in the Charles St. Jail, maybe scrubbing floors, mending clothing or taking in washing.

People's parties

Bars in rough neighborhoods often proved to be a safer gathering place than private parties. Parties did provide a social alternative for gay people—particularly lesbians—who were tired of dealing with the unwanted advances from straight men that often took place in bars. Yet while payoffs to the vice squad brought a certain amount of peace of mind for bar patrons, self-appointed moralists often provided the police with information about the private lives of their neighbors, resulting in subsequent raids and arrests. If charges were pressed, the names and addresses of attendees would be printed in the newspapers. The following excerpt describes an infamous raid on a private party held at 126 Commonwealth Avenue in March 1945:

"A whole slew of them"

I went to an evening party. The guy who owned [the place] had the most magnificent collection of records that you ever saw, and a fine phonograph. There were people from show business there. There was a young lady who danced in veils on a big, giant coffee table. It was so crowded.... People were just dancing and mingling and kissing and so forth. I was palling around with a Navy officer. I think we'd been there about two hours when the policemen arrived. A whole slew of them came dashing up the stairs. Afterwards we found out there'd been a plainclothesman at the party the whole time.

We all wound up at the Charles St. jail. I don't know how many of us...over twenty. We were there overnight.... I was working for a company that did advertising at the time. At the court trial, they mentioned that I was working at [name of company] and that they certainly wouldn't want people like me working there. I left. I just didn't go back [to work]. Too much publicity.

They just took it upon themselves—no search warrant or anything. They presumed there was something illegal

An illustration of the
courtroom trial following
the infamous party at 126
Commonwealth Avenue.
The man in the dock is
implicating one of the
defendants. Bob R.,
who provided the accom-
panying oral history,
is depicted wearing a
bow tie.

"And, your Honor, that person said to me, 'You are my lust.'"

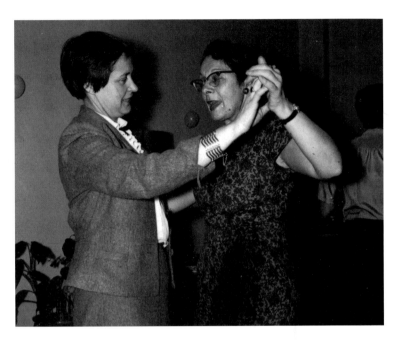

New Year's Eve, 1958

"A distinct absence of rhinestones"

The *Mid-Town Journal,* with its insatiable appetite for scandal, introduced its story about the raid with the headline, "Gay Ones Let Hair Down in Mad Court 'Orchid Festival.'" In describing the trial hearing, the *Journal's* reporter noted that "there was a distinct absence of rhinestones, heels and ostrich feathers. But the hearing was very gay—and so were the defendants."

A note found in the records of the Watch and Ward Society suggests collaboration with the vice squad:

or immoral going on so they had the opportunity to do as they pleased... and they did.

The aftermath of the raid at 126 Commonwealth was devastating. People all over the city just didn't want to go to parties. It reverberated throughout the bars.[8]
—Bob R.

After long painstaking investigation by the Secretary of the Watch and Ward, the "love nest" of homos was raided at 126 Commonwealth Avenue by the Vice Squad. 16 men and 2 women were arrested—all guilty on morals charges—and given probation by Judge Keniston.

Noted that: It is unfortunate that our Judges cannot or will not impose substantial fines and sentences upon these perverts.[9]

"Dykes in high heels"

Twelve years later, in 1957, private parties were still being raided:

We had a party up on Beacon Hill one night that got raided. The headline [in the *Mid-Town Journal*] was "Butch Balls Baffle Bulls." I left right before it got raided, but I went to court when they were arraigned the next morning. Well, you've never seen so many dykes in high heels in your life. The police didn't know what to do. Everybody was in their dyke clothes. They were giving phony names. [The police] had no complaint, so they had to drop it.[10]
—Alice F.

The *Journal* account mentioned in the previous excerpt appeared on 15 November 1957:

Butch Balls Baffle Bulls: Wild Whoopie Party Clinks Dozen Hefty Beacon Hill Babes.

Twenty husky gals with crew cuts, wearing dungarees and sweat shirts drunk, says police sergeant in raid.

Testifying at the trial [the sergeant said] that there were only one or two dim lights in the apartment and twenty girls, or maybe more, [who] were

were all drunk. He related that he had hauled six of the females out of the party and put them in a patrol wagon....

Questioned by the defense attorney and asked if the three defendants were drunk when he saw them in the apartment, Sgt. Devins stated everyone in the apartment was drunk and he couldn't tell one from the other.

Asked if a girl who had been arrested could walk a straight line, Sgt. Devin testified, "I don't know, I didn't have a line, but my eyesight is 20/20 and I could see her stagger."

Marion, a blonde, testified that she attended the party. When the policeman entered…"[he] told me I could leave as I was sober. I went to the station with two of my girl friends to bail our friends out and they brought us into the station and placed us under arrest. I asked them what I was being charged with," she informed the court, "and one of the officers told me I was charged with eating crackers in bed."

"It was really alluring to go to these places. The taboo was fascinating. It made you want to go out more. It was almost intoxicating."

—Robert G.

"It was exciting—kind of like a secret society. It was really different from what it is now. These gatherings felt sort of safe, even though you were always feeling that you had to hide yourself."

—Joy B.

Opposite:
"Gay Times Square"
(lower Washington
Street)

Haymarket Sq

SCOLLAY
SQUARE

Cambridge St

Bowdoin Sq

BEACON
HILL

Joy St

Myrtle St

Post Offi
Sq

Beacon St

Tremont St

"GAY TIMES
SQUARE"

Essex St

Commonwealth Av

Boylston St

Park Sq

BACK BAY

Eliot St

Kneeland St

Wasington St

Harrison Av

Copley Sq

Berkeley St

Columbus Av

Arlington St

Stuart St

BAY
VILLAGE

Tremont St

Broadway

SOUTH
COVE

Huntington Av

SOUTH END

Shawmut Av

Map of bars and gathering places, 1920–1960

▼ Gay bars
49 Cavana's*
61 Charlie Trafton's
   After Hours
48 Hotel St. Moritz/
   Vicki's*
42 Jacques*
25 Jazz Box
10 Jewel Box
41 Mario's/
   Sail Aweigh Bar
54 Midtown*
45 Napoleon Club*
38 The Other Side*
23 Petty Lounge*
27 Playland*
40 Punch Bowl*
 2 Sporter's*
44 Twelve Carver*

▽ Mixed crowd
18 Buddie's Club
15 Casa Blanca
11 Crawford House/
   Tally Ho
35 College Inn*
16 Half Dollar Bar
 1 Harvard Gardens
34 Hillbilly Ranch
22 Hotel Touraine
   Chess Room*
26 Izzy Orts
50 Kit Kat
12 Lighthouse
 8 Lincolnshire Hotel
53 Mardi Gras
59 Monarch Club
29 Novelty Bar
57 Rex
52 Rio Casino
14 Royal Café
 3 The Sevens
28 Silver Dollar*
30 Touraine Café*

☐ Speakeasies
 5 Brick Oven Tea
   Room
47 Empty Barrel
 6 Joy Barn
 4 March Hare
46 Nest
17 Pen and Pencil

● Restaurants
58 Child's*
32 Hayes Bickford*
51 Hayes Bickford*
24 Essex Deli
39 Jo's Steakhouse
37 Jo Bet's Restaurant
56 Melody Bar
   Restaurant
43 'Nineties
33 Nino Biaggi's
 7 Sharaf's
20 Tremont Plaza
21 Waldorf Cafeteria*

○ Baths
36 Lundin's Turkish
   Baths*

■ Hotels
 9 Hotel Imperial
55 Hotel Roosevelt
60 Irvington Rooms for
   Men

♦ Theaters
31 Stuart Theater*
13 Rialto*
19 Tivoli

Locations mentioned on the following
pages are marked with an asterisk (*).

The geography of a subculture

The preceding map indicates dozens of locations where gay people congregated in the years between Prohibition and Stonewall. Boston's gay subculture had begun to take shape during the speakeasy era, when the clandestine nature of illegal watering holes made them logical gathering places for people who saw themselves as marginalized. After the repeal of Prohibition, dozens of hotel lounges, former speakeasies, neighborhood bars, and nightclubs were frequented by a gay clientele, along with a number of hotels, restaurants, theaters, and bathhouses.

Bars and other gathering places gave previously isolated individuals the opportunity to experience a modicum of freedom, which helped to offset the constant threat of arrest, extortion, or loss of employment and the strain of leading double lives. Men and women who were usually segregated by gender, race, class, or lifestyle came together in the neighborhoods of Bay Village, Washington Street, Beacon Hill, and Scollay Square, where what they shared often outweighed their differences. The owners of these bars, who were both gay and straight, served as early leaders of the community, providing support and protection for customers. Bar raids were relatively infrequent, due to payoffs to police and the connections that many bar owners had to organized crime. One former bar employee describes this ritualized graft:

Every Saturday night, like clockwork, the vice squad would come in and take the entire Saturday night's receipts.... I went around with a paper bag to the three cash registers and put everything in. They'd have a drink and walk out with the cash.
—Alice F.

Of the more than sixty venues indicated on the map, only a handful are still in operation. Many were destroyed during urban renewal in the 1960s. In some ways, the map serves as a testament to a dynamic and diverse subculture that existed before the Stonewall riots.

In the recollections presented on the following pages, references to map locations are indicated by their corresponding numbers on the map key; for example, the number "22" refers to the Chess Room at the Hotel Touraine.

"A secret society"

Given the relative freedom now enjoyed by many lesbians and gay men, it is easy to forget that just a few decades ago, gay culture was virtually invisible to "mainstream" society. This repression took its toll in the form of suicides, alcoholism, unhappy marriages, and the lowering of career aspirations. At the same time, the risks and dangers for lesbians and gay men were often tinged with excitement.

One lesbian recalls the effect that this heady, illicit atmosphere had on gay women, who had fewer options than men when it came to meeting in public places:

It always felt like being in a private club, because in those days nobody knew. You could hide. We used to say that it was a special thing about being a lesbian. You had little signals that you'd give to each other, and you could identify each other with your antenna, but nobody else knew. So, when you did find somebody else, it was exciting—kind of like a secret society. It was really different from what it is now. These gatherings felt sort of safe, even though you were always feeling that you had to hide yourself.[11]
—Joy B.

163

Left above:
Girl's night out at Playland, c.1959

Left below:
A group of friends at Playland, 1959

Some men experienced a similar thrill at the prospect of meeting others like themselves:

It was exciting at dusk to start to get ready to go out because you knew you were going to meet a man or pick up a man. It was really alluring to go to these places. The taboo was fascinating. It made you want to go out more. It was almost intoxicating.
—Robert G.

From the Cold War to Stonewall: 1945–1969

Gay Times Square

"Gay Times Square" was the name given to a span of lower Washington Street that was home to a number of gathering places. A coat and tie were required for entrance to the Chess Room at the Touraine Hotel (22); the Touraine Café (30) was, according to one patron, an "upholstered sewer" where prostitutes, strippers, and drunks mixed with gay men and a few lesbians. Lower Washington Street later became the Combat Zone, a center for strip joints and porn theaters abutting Boston's Chinatown. The Zone was eventually cleaned up, leaving Playland (27) as its sole survivor.[12]

Silver Dollar, c. 1958

Silver Dollar (28)

In its heyday during the 1930s and 1940s, the Silver Dollar boasted enormous crowds, the longest bar in the country, and its own radio station on the premises. During World War II, the bar was a favorite of soldiers and sailors. Gay men looking to meet men in uniform had to be extremely discreet or risk being thrown out. After the war, the Silver Dollar had a brief stint as a gay bar.

There were a lot of married guys that went in there. It was absolutely safe; I never remember a fight. Servicemen [went there] during the war, and after the war there were still a lot of people in the service. Later, when most of the service people were gone, it was all gay people in civilian clothes. Everybody dressed up to go in there… penny loafers, gaberdine slacks, sweaters, tweed jackets, and colored shirts [which] had just come in.[13]
—Mr. G.

Playland (27)

Boston's oldest gay bar, established in 1938, Playland came to be viewed as an alternative to the "piss-elegant" Napoleon Club (45). In its early years, the bar featured a mural that showed Playland regulars mingling with movie stars. There was also a balcony that saw performances by an assortment of dancers, singers, and show people. The bar still draws the city's most eclectic crowd by age, class, race, and dress size.

Playland (right), c. 1980

Playland's owners found a way to sidestep Boston's blue laws, which went into effect at midnight on Saturday night and prohibited patrons from drinking at the bar until Monday. Employees who opened the bar on Sundays would place boards across the barstools and set up folding chairs for the customers. In this way, the police couldn't fine the owners, since no drinking took place at the actual bar.

"A lonely petunia"

Jim McGrath worked as a bartender at Playland for thirty-eight years. McGrath's contributions included elaborate decorating schemes for Independence Day, Halloween, and other holidays. McGrath also helped to institute a Thanksgiving dinner for patrons and neighbors, a tradition that continues to the present day. Mary Brown, a waitress and singer at the club, was a heterosexual woman who served as a mother figure for many gay men. Her routine included songs like "I'm a Lonely Petunia in an Onion Patch."

Marie Cord was a lesbian singer and burlesque performer who frequented the club.

Marie Cord had beautiful red hair. Her lover was mannish. [The lover] wore her hair in a man's haircut. She went to a barber shop, and wore men's suits and ties. This is how many lesbians looked at the time. They would wear shirts and ties, and take on the stance of men.

Marie was from Boston. She had gone to Hollywood, where she had a few bit parts. Whatever happened, she never made it. She was a singer. Everywhere she went, as soon as she walked in, everybody would request one of her songs, "Love Is Just A Game," and she would sing it.
—Robert G.

Bartender Jim McGrath (center) with Ray Kennard (left) and a singer named Harold. Ray played piano at Playland in the 1950s and 1960s. Harold sang to Ray's accompaniment; his signature songs were "Always" and "The More I See You." He was murdered leaving Napoleon's in 1966.

Above:
Marie Cord

Right:
Rialto Theater, c. 1958

Above:
Playland waitress Mary
Brown performing, 1959

Petty Lounge (23)

My boyfriend Freddy and I went over there because we heard that they didn't mind boys who were homosexual. When we went in, we were kind of nervous, until the waitress bounced up and said, "Are you boys gay?" We were shocked, and sort of stuttered and stammered. She said, "Oh, I just want to know because we have special prices for gay boys." That was back in 1950.
—Preston C.

Stuart Theater (31)
Rialto Theater (13)

I met a lot of people in the movies. The Stuart was the gay theater.... The management knew what was going on. You could have sex in the men's room or in the seats. There was another theater in Scollay Square—the Rialto. I met some wonderful people in there. A lot of very butch straight men would go for a little relaxation and to meet someone. You saw two full length features, the news, coming attractions, and serials all for a quarter. You could be there all day. Where could you ever find a bargain like that today?
—Mr. G.

The logo for the Napoleon Club

Ads for Cavana's and Lundin's Turkish Baths from the *Mid-Town Journal*

Bay Village, South Cove, and Park Square

After the war, much of Boston's gay activity migrated from Washington Street to the Bay Village/South Cove area. At one time, gay people could socialize at almost twenty different establishments. Broadway and Carver Street boasted a particularly high concentration of gathering places—from Lundin's Turkish Baths to Cavana's, an early women's bar. Most of these were destroyed as a result of urban renewal. The area was also home to drag queens, transvestite hustlers, and other distinctive personalities.

One resident was Jimmy Gaines, a black, ex-drag queen entertainer who...was flagrant as flagrant can be. When he wasn't working, he would hang out his front window with his elbows on the sill and call, "Yoohoo!" to all the truck drivers.... One Halloween, Jimmy invited us to come down to watch him get dressed in full drag. We [expected] it would just be his gay friends. When we got there, we were flabbergasted to find that not only his gay friends were there, but his brothers and sisters, his nieces and nephews, who were there to see Uncle Jimmy [become] Aunt Jimmy.[14]
—Barbara H.

Napoleon Club (45)

Still in operation, Napoleon's opened as a speakeasy in 1929. It operated as a private club with a sizable gay clientele. Under new ownership in 1952, it became a gay bar.

Long after [the Napoleon's] days as a speakeasy, patrons had to push a buzzer and be viewed through a peephole. If they knew you, they'd let you in. You had to be dressed in a tie and coat and jacket. For a long time they didn't allow women, and when they did they couldn't wear pants.
—Bob R.

Napoleon's piano bar was decorated with bold black-and-red decor, and a collection of Napoleonic artifacts and motifs. Every patron had a favorite piano player:

At the Napoleon Club there was a black piano player by the name of Sidney. Next to him there was a beautiful lamp of a Nubian slave holding a fan.... He looked like Bobby Short. He sang upstairs and had a very large clientele.
—Robert G.

Top:
The Punch Bowl (right),
c. 1958. Mario's (41) is to
the left.

Bottom:
Tremont Street at night,
c. 1958. Cavana's is at
the extreme left. The St.
Moritz Hotel (home of
Vicki's) is two doors to
the right of Cavana's.

Punch Bowl (40)

One of the most popular bars of the 1950s and 1960s, the Punch Bowl (formerly Phil Harris') entertained huge crowds—and, on many occasions, the vice squad:

About once a night they would flash the emergency lights, which meant that the vice were coming and you had to stop dancing with your boyfriend, since it was illegal back then. You could dance with a lesbian, or you could sit down.
—Preston C.

"The Irish girls called it Cavanaugh's"

A 1962 *Mid-Town Journal* profile described Cavana's (49) as

the bistro where muscular amazons, who could punch as hard as Popeye after he had eaten three cans of spinach, would cuddle blonde cuties on their laps as they guzzled boilermakers.

There seated in booths, perched on stools at the bar, and milling about were females, some blondes, brunettes, some with whiffle hair cuts, some with exquisite, long tresses. Some wore wranglers trousers, some dungarees, some wore dresses, but males were few and far between, and other than the bartender and the cook, females dominated the scene.

Two women describe the route to Cavana's lesbian back room:

You walked through a front room [full of workmen] in uniforms.... They didn't touch you, but it was like walking the gauntlet. They were always saying things like, "I can do it better than your girlfriend."[15]
—Helaine Z.

The front room of the bar was this collection of guys who were largely fish queens—men who were interested in trying to have sex with a lesbian. Slimiest group of men you've ever encountered..... The back room was the entire spectrum of the lesbian community, from the college kids with their dirty Bermuda shorts to old dykes with their wives, presided over by Esther. Esther was built like a fire plug, had a mouth like a sewer, and the personality of a pit bull. She was not lovely.... If anybody got thrown out, it was Esther who threw you out.
—Barbara H.

Vicki's (48)

Vicki's was located at the Hotel St. Moritz on Tremont Street:

Vicki was a big dyke who was probably in her forties then. Vicki would sit on a big high stool in the back room and kind of give you the eye. We would go in there, a whole group of us. [The other patrons] would look at us like, "Who is the butch, and who is the fem?" They thought we were quite suspect. We had all been to college and they were all working in factories. At the drop of a hat they'd throw a beer bottle across the room, so we were a little bit uptight about them.
—Helaine Z.

"The women would be taken off in private cars"

One woman provides a harrowing account of police harassment at the Midtown (54):

It was really scary and very intense to go down there. Nick sat on a barstool next to the door. When the vice squad raided [the bar] he'd lean against the wall, and the lights would go on downstairs. When the lights went on, the same-sex dancers would either grab someone [of the opposite sex], or you'd stop dancing, because it was against the law.

They'd come down and everybody would line up against the wall. You had to show that you had money or you'd be picked up for vagrancy. If you didn't have the money, you'd be arrested.... The men would be taken off in [the Black Maria] and the women would be taken off in private cars. Most of the men didn't get to jail without some rough stuff. If the women came back in a short period of time, that meant a blow job and no arrest. It was sort of humiliating for the women to come back to the other women because we would know. It was the lesser of two evils, because otherwise you would get arrested and have a record. It was very, very sad. There was not a thing you could do about it.

When they would go around checking the ID's, if the name was prominent you would be subject to blackmail. Penny ante shit—$25. It was a very tough time. It's a wonder we didn't all go straight.
—Alice F.

"The mother of us all"

Tex's first waitress job was at the Ritz. "Then she discovered the gay boys and she loved them." During her long career in gay bars, Tex worked at the Punch Bowl, Sporters (2), and several other bars. "Tex was the mother of us all," noted one patron. "If somebody was short before payday she'd lend him the money he needed. She was a good soul."[16]

Left:
Warrenton Street, c. 1958. Although already closed when this photograph was taken, the Midtown Rendezvous had been in the basement of what is now the Charles Playhouse.

Right:
Tex

Top:
**The Other Side (left)
and Jacques (right, with
awning),
c. 1969**

Bottom:
Phil Baione

Jacques (42) and
The Other Side (38)

Opened in 1938, Jacques became a gay bar in the mid-1940s. Its owner opened The Other Side in 1965, the first discotheque in the city to allow same-sex dancing. After serving as the city's only lesbian bar from the late 1960s to the early 1970s, Jacques evolved into a venue for drag performers, which remains its focus to the present day. The Other Side closed in 1976, due to noise complaints from neighbors.

Phil Baione

Owner of Twelve Carver in Boston and Wuthering Heights in Provincetown, Phil Baione was a bar manager who also entertained:

He would come out in drag, only the drag was just in the front. It would be a gown, but it would be tied around him like an apron. From the back you could see the men's clothes. He would come down on a red velvet swing in a huge hat and a beaded bag. His hat was often two huge doves—when he pulled a string, the wings would open. He weighed over three hundred pounds. You'd be sitting there, thinking, "If that swing ever breaks, we'll all be goners."
—Robert G.

Lundin's Turkish Baths (36)

Lundin's was in operation from 1903 until the 1960s. For years it operated with both men's and women's sections, but only the men's area was open all night. One patron remembers:

Oh, Lundin's! I had a wonderful time there. Sometimes I'd spend the whole day, or I'd stay over another day and never leave. It was like dying and going to heaven.... You'd put your clothes in the locker and put a sheet around your waist. They had a swimming pool there, immaculately clean. You would sit around the pool nude or with a towel. They were all gay there, or straight people looking for gay times. You'd meet around the pool, then you had your room. You'd lay in your bed and pose as attractive as you could. This was serious stuff. They would peek in and if they liked what they saw, you would tell them to come in. Then you'd jump in the shower or in the pool and come out again ready for another round. It was lovely; it was perfectly safe. That was before the epidemic.

—Mr. G.

Hayes Bickford, corner of Tremont and Boylston Streets, 1965

Hayes Bickford Restaurants (32, 51)
Child's (58)
Waldorf Cafeteria (21)

Restaurants served as gathering places for teenagers who were too young to gain admittance to bars, and for the after-hours bar crowd. The Hayes Bickford restaurants were located on Tremont Street and in Park Square (the latter was known as the "Gay Hayes"). Both locations drew huge numbers of late-night revelers. The Waldorf Cafeteria was the "Gay Apple." According to one patron, "The Apple was for people who wanted to relax; the Hayes was for those with a touch of madness."

Top:
Bob White (right) with Charlie Trafton, who ran a boarding house and after-hours club out of his St. Botolph Street home for about forty years. Liberace, Anthony Perkins, and Judy

Garland were all reported to have visited Trafton's home after performances.

Bottom:
Like many gay bars, the facade of Sporter's was unmarked.

Beacon Hill

Before and after the Second World War, the north slope of Beacon Hill was a rooming-house district that attracted an eclectic, largely bohemian crowd. Located near Scollay Square, the Hill became a popular residence for lesbians and gay men, who gathered at Harvard Gardens (1), The Sevens (3), Sharaf's (7), and other bars and restaurants.

Sporter's (2)

Celebrated in John Reid's 1973 novel *The Best Little Boy in the World,* Sporter's opened in 1939 as a neighborhood bar. Lesbians and gay men began to frequent the bar in the 1950s. In 1957, Bob White persuaded the owner to make the Beacon Hill bar "officially" gay, since much of the regular clientele was gay. After White became the manager, some say that he instituted a policy of making lesbians wear dresses to discourage them from returning. The bar benefited from the demolition of Scollay Square in the 1960s, when customers from bars in the Square began to patronize Sporter's. White went on to "convert" other Boston bars, as well as the suburban Randolph Country Club. Sporter's closed its doors in 1995.

It was just a neighborhood bar but, as people started moving to the Hill, they started going there. The Sevens on the other side of the Hill—Charles Street—was too obviously straight and collegiate, and Sporter's wasn't.... All the old derelicts from Scollay Square would wander down to Sporter's. We had the Opera Lady. She would just sit there until she got good and shit-faced, and then she'd sing along with the jukebox in a high, operatic voice. We had the Old Man—this guy with long, shaggy hair and a big beard. Marguerite was the waitress; she was fun. Of course, she loved the gay crowd because we tipped her. The other set didn't tip, so she was much happier when we took it over.
—Alice F.

Fear, isolation—and community

In the years between World War II and Stonewall—despite persecutions ranging from police harassment and societal oppression to physical assault, extortion, and even murder—lesbians and gay men continued to find each other. The following quotations provide a reminder of the nature of gay life in the years before the liberation movement.

My taste was in real super butch men, and most of them were married. I used to like them big and rugged—6 feet 4 and 250 pounds and no fat, but looked like professional wrestlers. That was my type and somehow they liked me. I was sort of delicate, feminine. They were all married, that was my trouble. I wanted to settle down with one person; I wanted to hook up with somebody, but everybody that I liked was married and they didn't want to break up their home. I knew some of them for 30 years.
—Mr. G.

Right, above and below: John (left) and Robert were lovers who operated a service station in Belmont during the 1950s. John is seen below with the couple's Airedales.

Opposite: Joy B., c. 1955

People would go to the Hotel Roosevelt for cheap rooms. One night I was waiting for the elevated at the Dover Street stop. I can remember seeing a black man and a white man embracing in the window. It gave me such a warm feeling to see that.
—Robert G.

Early on [in the late 1930s], I thought I was the only gay person, then later on I found I wasn't. Then, I thought I was the only gay Jewish man, and I found out that wasn't so. When I got to dental school, I thought I was the only gay, Jewish dentist—which wasn't so either. You eventually found out that you were not alone.
—Chester S.[17]

Everybody was in the closet. You had to hide it. You had to be a good actor. You'd say that you were separated, or that you were married but not living together, or you were getting a divorce. The word "gay" was our secret word. Up until 1953 or 1954 the straights really didn't know what "gay" meant. So, you'd be in a group of people, and you would lean over to someone and whisper, "Are you gay?"
—Conrad S.

We had a sense of humor that didn't quit, even in the face of adversity. There was always a lot of humor, almost in a classic kind of way, with all the tragedy. There were many women who would have done different things with their lives but, for fear of scandal, they couldn't. They didn't take chances—whether that would be different professions, higher education, or higher visibility. They would take hidden jobs. We didn't know many women who went into higher education or the professions. Many women got married; some married gay men. You were always subject to termination, there was no question about that. There was no question of violating your rights, because you didn't have any.

You always had two sets of clothes, two sets of friends. We had good times, but it was real stressful. I don't think most people could really understand unless you lived through those times—the distaste that people expressed about queers. A mass murderer or a serial killer would be a rung above us.

—Alice F.

From the Cold War to Stonewall: 1945–1969

Drag under fire

Drag queens and cross-dressing women were responsible for some of the earliest acts of resistence by lesbians and gay men. Until 1948, drag performances were an accepted part of Boston nightlife. The College Inn pushed the limits of social acceptability by having both performers and waiters appear in drag. These singing waiters, who served up risqué songs while sitting on the laps of male customers, drew enormous crowds that often included Hollywood personalities.

This was enough for the Boston Licensing Board to rule that the College Inn could no longer operate unless the staff wore proper clothing. Police harassment of the workers followed. They were placed under surveillance, and some were arrested in their homes for being "lewd persons." Six-month sentences at Deer Island, a correctional institution located in Boston Harbor, were handed out routinely for this charge. By all accounts, this purge, which continued throughout the 1950s, led to an exodus from Boston.

True to form, the *Mid-Town Journal* kept close tabs on the scandal, as in this excerpt dated 22 October 1948:

Boys Mustn't Dress As Girls in Barroom Licensing Board Rules; College Inn Cited

The College Inn at Albany Street and Broadway…last week had its entertainment license suspended after investigators testified before the City of Boston Licensing Board that males…were dressed as girls and waited on tables while they gave out with risqué ditties, much to the delight of the patrons. The Board, after issuing a suspension decree, ordered the manager to put pants on his men, and if they were girls to make them wear dresses.

The *Journal* was still pursuing similar stories in May 1949:

Cerise Drapes Drop On Lavender Lads As Cops Clean Up Boston Queers

They danced in quadrille in the tea room,
and screamed several shades of cerise;
The molls were ringing,
  the belles were singing;
"Down with the chief of police!"

A mad clicking of rhinestone heels and hurried packing of hennaed switches, ostrich plumes and strapless evening gowns is going on in Boston!... The Licensing Board and the Police Department are hotspotting a crusade to ban female impersonators from Hub nighteries, as an overture to rid the city of Subway Sammies and numerous other undesirable homosexuals.... No stone will be unturned—and no alleyway or tramway tea room unexplored—police say, in their campaign to preserve the purity of the City of Culture, which has lately been tagged as a wide-open "Harlequinesque Fairyland."

It came to a head when Rosco Pallideno, thrilled at the brisk business his College Inn on Albany Street was doing, bought the Mayfair Night Club on Broadway, remodelled it extensively, and was preparing to transfer the whole kit and boodle, faggy waiters and all, uptown, when the Boston Licensing Board stepped in and said: "WHOA!" And it issued orders to the Police Department that "no innholder, common victualler, or person owning, managing or controlling a cafe, restaurant, or other eating or drinking establishment shall permit on the licensed premises the impersonation of a female by a male entertainer, or by male employees of the licensee, nor shall any male employee impersonate a female as a master of ceremonies, hostess, waitress, or in any other way whatsoever.

So, that's that! And now the only way those so inclined may swish and flit around in blonde wigs and sequin gowns will be on Hallowe'en!—or in the Hasty Pudding Shows. Wiseacres and old-time gay boys who have since withdrawn from active participation on the local scene, shake their heads knowingly, and murmur: "Yes, Julia, the time has come!" And they sadly go back to their hem-stitching as they reminisce how gay Boston used to be in the "good old days."

A 1952 advertisement for the College [Inn] Cafe. Other ads promoted the fact that the club featured "Singing Waiters—New York Style."

A shutter from the Kit-Kat Club on Fayette Street, which now hangs on the house next door.

The author goes on to invoke a number of venues that had already vanished from the landscape:

There are those who remember when Dixie Fay swished around for several consecutive years at the **Silver Dollar;** when Millie, Nora Ford, Edna Guertin, *et al*, can-canned in "drag" at the old **Hotel Roosevelt** opposite Rowe's Wharf; when Mother Green held forth at the **Village Barn;** and when the belles were ringing wildly in such mad local spots as the **Tally-Ho,** the **Blackstone Tap,** the **Tivoli** and the **Miami Grove.**

Then there are those ancient ones who recall the **"Nest,"** the **"Empty Barrel"** and the **"Kit Kat Club"** in Kerry Village [Bay Village].

All that is over now. All the pet rendezvous of the lavender lads will be strictly "jam," as of immediately, the Police Department threatens. And habitués of such bistros as **Playland, the Green Cafe, Phil Harris',** the **Napoleon Club** and the **Red Shutter** in East Boston will have to take their darning and knitting elsewhere, to reform and get stiff in the same dignified, orthodox manner as their normal fellow roustabouts.

Before concluding with a meditation on gay life that brings together characters as diverse as Oscar Wilde, Walt Whitman, and Julian Eltinge, the author makes a series of observations that, coming twenty years prior to the Stonewall riots, seem eerily prescient:

All this presents a complex problem for the reformers who wish to eradicate what has become a national plague.… What to do with these thousands and thousands of young men who suddenly realize they aren't interested in women…only the clothes they wear? What to do with more than a million homosexuals swishing unrestrained throughout America? The solution to the problem is not as simple as it seems, when it is considered that many of these "queers" are strictly undercover, and defy detection because they are presumably respectable businessmen, artists, lawyers, and athletes.…

This is not a new situation. It had early beginnings in ancient Greece when the lifting up of a toga, accompanied by a daring grope and a peek, was considered a popular, everyday past time, and up through the ages, during which time such people as Oscar Wilde, William Shakespeare and Walt Whitman were accused of being "gay." And it was only a couple decades ago that the "Queen" of them all, Julian Eltinge, knocked many men down when they accused him of being a wee bit odd, accumulated an envious fortune by his female impersonations and shocked ladies' aid societies and bewildered adolescents from coast to coast with a daring movie, "Maid to Order."

Bridgeport or Bust

In 1952 Captain G. F. Caswell published *Boston: Today,* a serviceman's guide to the seamier side of the city's night life. The nightclub Caswell refers to in the first paragraph is the College Inn. The "joint" near Washington and Essex Streets is Playland:

For a while, Boston was headquarters for these people who are different— men who acted like women, women who acted like men, and some who acted like nothing else. They even had their own night club in the heart of the city: and probably more of the general public patronized it than any other nightclub in town. The shows were good and not as offensive as some in other ordinary places. But the boys in the show wore girls' blouses and had fancy hairdos. And the waiters had high voices and wore lipstick.

So, they took off the skirts, put on slacks, and moved into one of the better club locations right downtown; and the place was more of a success than the old one. Then many, many

months later, a local keeper-of-the-morals brought about a general "cleanup" of the city's shows. Something happened and the above club closed. The "people" mostly left town and headed for more appreciative places like Bridgeport.

Now we are relatively free of them (though a couple of joints near Washington and Essex still see many around) and hope we remain that way.[18]

Drag queen at Playland, 1959

Profile:
Sylvia Sidney

Above:
Sylvia Sidney, age five. "My mother used to dress me up like a little girl with long curls. I thought I was a girl. In pretty little outfits, not dresses. I didn't know there was a difference between a girl and a boy."

Right:
Sylvia as a waiter in the 1940s

Sylvia Sidney, Boston's most (in)famous drag queen, has described himself as "a fun-loving, outspoken homosexual who speaks his mind—and if people don't like it, the hell with them, my dear." He began his career as a drag performer in 1947, at the age of seventeen:

I'm not considered a drag queen *per se*, trying to impersonate another woman. You've never seen a woman that looked like me! I look more like a hard-core madam, sort of a Mae West caricature. When I hit the stage I'm coarse, loud, and vulgar.[19]

Sylvia received his stage name one day in the 1940s while walking through the Public Garden.

I went down to what they call Queen's Row in the Public Garden. It was a dirt road. They had benches. Some older queens were there. They said, "Oh, hi honey! How are you? Aren't you cute!" I wasn't really cute at all. They said, "What's your name?" I said, "My name is Sidney." They said, "We'll call you Sylvia." They called everybody a name. There was a Bette Davis, there was a Helen Morgan. There was a queen who looked like Katharine Hepburn. She had a twin brother—the Hepburn sisters.

For his first performance, Sylvia stepped out on stage wearing purple lounging pajamas with white polka dots and sang, "Kiss me sweet, kiss me simple, kiss me on my lips." Patrons of the Rex, a straight club, booed him off the stage. As Sylvia tells it, local piano virtuoso Jerry Whiting found him backstage crying. Whiting told him to go back out, pick up the microphone, and say whatever was on his mind. Sylvia went back out for a second show and let loose with a string of expletives that wouldn't quit. The audience started throwing money and cheering. The manager offered him five dollars for three shows a night, and a career was born.

Left:
Sylvia wearing cucumber earrings and necklace in Provincetown during the 1960s

Right:
Sylvia in a mirrored gown

184

Charlie Titus as Marie Antoinette

The Statler, Sherry-Biltmore, and Ritz-Carlton Hotels all hosted the drag Beaux Arts Ball, an annual extravaganza that was staged on a regular basis until the late 1960s. Hundreds of people came from as far away as New York, Chicago, and Florida to attend the ball. Kleig lights and limousines announced the attendees to the crowds who lined the streets to catch a glimpse of the elaborate costumes. Each year featured a different theme— "A Night at the Opera," "Kings and Queens," or "Black and White."[20]

One friend went as the opera, *The Love of Three Oranges.* He was dressed in a yellow chiffon gown and his hair was sprayed gold. He had made a large pumpkin; his lover put him on a dolly and pulled him on stage in this big pumpkin. A big puff of smoke came out of the pumpkin and out jumped my friend in this one-shouldered chiffon gown with gold ankle-straps and gold hair. He came in second. First place was won by Charlie Titus. He had gone as Marie Antoinette. He had a big white pompadour, and inside there was a birdcage with two love birds.

Everyone had limousines. They dropped you off at the front door of the hotel…. The doorman opened the car and you'd see these beautifully gowned women coming out. Of course they were men, with their escorts. People passing by would think it was a Hollywood premier. There wasn't anything cheap about it. Some of those gay people would be sewing all year long. They'd be at the beach in Provincetown sewing this crepe. You'd know exactly what they were doing. They were getting ready for October.

—Robert G.

Each year they had a theme. The opera, musicals, or literature. It was quasi-intellectual. It was all men. Probably some women went, but I didn't know any. Absolutely breathtaking. I remember thinking how exciting it was to be a part of that group, even though it was secret. Traffic would be blocked. There were hundreds of people on the street watching. I didn't notice anyone on the streets with signs or picketing or anything. There would be applause for the costumes. Those queens. They loved it. I remember the year the theme was "A Night at the Opera." There were dozens of Madame Butterfly's.

—Alice F.

**Beaux Arts Ball attendee,
c. 1955**

Provincetown

Provincetown's reputation as an art colony extended back to the turn of the century. In the years between World War II and Stonewall, increasing numbers of gay people began to view Provincetown as a destination for those seeking new faces and more anonymity, in a setting known for natural beauty of all kinds:

I remember going to Provincetown for the first time, perhaps around 1953. I can remember that when I appeared on the beach, people were getting up and applauding. I was looking behind me thinking, "I wonder who they're applauding for?" When I asked the man I was with, he said, "They're clapping at you, because they know you're a new face in town." —Robert G.

The official start of the summer season at Herring Cove Beach in Provincetown was marked by the arrival of Phil Baione, owner and manager of the Wuthering Heights bar in Provincetown and Twelve Carver in Boston. The crowd never knew whether Phil would arrive in a helicopter or in a speedboat accompanied by Sylvia Sidney. What they could count on was that his entrance would be spectacular:

Phil Baione was a very large man, a gregarious, loud, outgoing kind of person—great flair, great warmth. He loved being "on" and performed all the time. In Provincetown at the beginning of the season he would arrive on the beach with picture hats and an entourage of boys. One time he came down from a helicopter. There was a flamboyance about him. He certainly had a show-the-world attitude. He had no qualms about hiding who he was. He would do imitations of celebrities in semi-drag on a swing in his club in Provincetown, Wuthering Heights. He would sit on the swing and do a show every afternoon in a hat with trailing ribbons. An amazing man.[21]
—Paul M.

Phil Baione on Herring
Cove Beach, c. 1952

Despite its reputation as a bohemian enclave, Provincetown wasn't always welcoming and carefree:

They had the Ten Commandments of Provincetown, where they wouldn't allow you to wear shorts above your knee, and if you had bleached hair you would be suspect. Two men couldn't share a room. If you were walking along the street and your arms touched, they would come by with a cruiser and take both of you and throw you in jail.
—Robert G.

**Kick line at Herring Cove
Beach, Provincetown,
1952**

Social worker Barbara
Hoffman (left) and
friends, 1958

Homophobia and urban renewal

In the 1950s and early 1960s, Boston was a city in decline on the verge of bankruptcy. Attempts at urban renewal destroyed many working-class and ethnically mixed neighborhoods. Boston's first experiment with urban renewal took place in the West End, prior to architectural preservation regulations. The wholesale destruction of the historic properties in this established neighborhood provoked a national scandal. Less is known about the extent to which urban renewal efforts were targeted toward Boston's lesbian and gay communities. What is certain is that by the late 1960s, Scollay Square, Bay Village, South Cove, and Park Square—all of which were widely frequented by gay men and lesbians—had been radically and irrevocably altered.[22]

At least one official, City Councillor Frederick "Freddy" Langone, was willing to endorse publicly the destruction of Boston's gay bars. What follows is an excerpt from Langone's remarks at a city council meeting on 7 July 1965:

Either we lick it, we will stop it, or let them continue to exist. We are now concerned with the South Cove area. I count at least four or five places where [gay bars] exist now, and one outside the area on Carver Street.... I am wondering now if we eliminate a half dozen of those places within the South Cove area, perhaps the youth of America in this area would be served better....

We will be better off without these incubators of homosexuality and indecency and a Bohemian way of life. I tell you right now, we will be better off without it and if we accomplish nothing else, at least we will uproot this cancer in one area of the city.[23]

Left:
The Crawford House in its heyday during the 1920s

Below:
Demolition of the Crawford House, Scollay Square, 1962

From the Cold War to Stonewall: 1945–1969

Tremont Street, Bay
Village, 1965. The block
shown, home to Cavana's
and Vicki's, is now occu-
pied by the Church of All
Nations.

This article from the *Mid-Town Journal* of 12 July 1965 describes the meeting in which Langone made his comments:

City Councillor Frederick C. Langone terminated his impressive speech at the council hearing with a hearty Langoneism that vibrated the rafters of the Old City Hall, as he expounded his views with, "We must uproot these joints so the innocent kids won't be contaminated."

After referring to the Park Square and Cove area as the Greenwich Village of Boston, which is about as much like Greenwich Village as the Kurile Islands, Langone continued blithely on during the hearing of the Council's Urban Renewal Committee on the fate of some thirty liquor establishments facing abolishment under the South Cove urban renewal plot....

Stating that it was disgusting to observe the actions of the limp wrist set on the sidewalks—so disgusting that it turned his delicate stomach—he demanded that the breeding grounds of homosexuals be demolished, as he sadly wondered what would happen to the future of America if sexual aberrations became a way of life in this great United States of ours, where there are only a few hundreds [of homosexuals] left working in government posts in Washington, a few thousand financiers, and maybe hundreds of small politicians scattered all over the country, that would total more than a million votes, which might come in handy if he ever decided to run for the presidency.

One thing his stirring speech did was to enlighten many who were unaware that Homosexuals arrive differently, in the respect that they are "incubated in the barrooms."

All in all the Cove area is in the bag and fags or no fags, it's going the way other sections of the City have gone—to make a great big new and vacant Boston.

Profile:
Prescott Townsend

Prescott Townsend could have boasted that twenty-three members of his family came over on the *Mayflower,* and that his ancestors signed the Declaration of Independence, the Articles of Confederation, and the Constitution. Instead, he routinely reported about his life as an activist for homosexual rights to his fellow Harvard graduates of the Class of 1918 in their annual reports. An excerpt from the forty-fifth anniversary report follows:

The third and last phase of my life has been the fight for social justice. This has also been the most fun. The Demophile Center is one of the three newer organizations in the United States dedicated to bringing the problems of the homophile to the attention of the public and aiding in their solution. I do this by my forensic and scriptural abilities, by my leadership of the Demophile, and also by membership in the international society.

Townsend's political organizing began several years before the formation of the Boston Demophile Center in 1962, with an effort to establish a Boston branch of the Mattachine Society in 1957. Townsend's activism may have been motivated by an eighteen-month jail term he received in 1943, which he served at the Massachusetts House of Corrections on Deer Island, for committing an "unnatural and lascivious act" with an eighteen-year-old man. Townsend cast the event differently in the fiftieth anniversary report:

**Prescott Townsend
in his youth**

I helped win the Incredible Battle of Midway by working two years down at Fore River with a shipfitter's wedge, one time at ten below zero. Then I was thrown in jail for refusing to pay [$1500 in] graft for an act that is not against the law in England nor in Illinois. I came out the day the war was over.

The *Mid-Town Journal* headline of 29 January 1943 reported, "Beacon Hill 'Twilight' Man Member of Queer Love Cult Seduced Young Man":

After calling for Townsend's record, the judge who sentenced him declared it was one of the worst records he had ever seen, and branded him an aggressor in leading men astray. Townsend, a husky, manly-appearing individual, who has been employed at the Fore River yard as a shipfitter, denied the charges and appealed the sentence.

Townsend's confrontational style rankled the New York members of the Mattachine Society. Prior to the first meeting of the Boston chapter in 1957, one New York representative wrote:

A duty which someone in your group will have to do before the…meeting is to visit all the psychology departments of the local universities, Harvard, Northeastern, Boston Univ. and ask for permission to place an announcement of the meeting on their bulletin board, together with a copy of "What Does Mattachine Do?". I believe they will grant permission, provided it isn't Townsend who tries to make the contact. I have my reservations how many speakers he will be able to get because of the bad impression he leaves.[24]

This statement may have been based on the fact that the owners of the hall secured for the first meeting canceled the reservation when Townsend told them that it was needed for a meeting of a "socio-sexual society."

A founding member of the Boston chapter wrote:

We shall have as little to do with Townsend as possible. We will certainly not alienate him, we will only try to keep him under control. The Boston group have been told to concentrate only on organizational matters, and forget about "launching out to fight for the cause."[25]

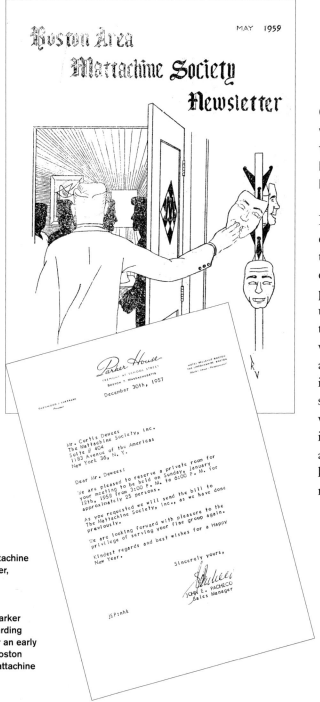

On 27 November 1959, Townsend wrote to Mattachine's New York chapter president, requesting support for his efforts in overturning the sodomy law. The president responded:

Let me say that I feel that it is still too early in the history of the Mattachine to sponsor a bill in a state legislature concerning change in the sex laws. I personally feel that we should wait until we have the support of psychiatrists, ministers, lawyers and others who could testify on behalf of such an action, and who could vouch for our integrity. We do not have that professional backing at this time. However, I would be very interested in seeing you introduce such a bill as an individual, and do hope you do so. I would like to know what sort of reaction it would receive.[26]

Above:
Boston Area Mattachine Society Newsletter, May 1959

Right:
Letter from the Parker House hotel regarding arrangements for an early meeting of the Boston chapter of the Mattachine Society in 1957

Opposite:
Prescott Townsend at home on Beacon Hill in the late 1960s

From the Cold War to Stonewall: 1945–1969

Setting the stage

By the 1960s, events in Boston, as in the rest of the United States, had radically challenged traditional notions of power and entitlement. The civil rights and black power movements, the Vietnam War, the youth culture, and the women's movement all contributed to this phenomenon. The hope for profound social change, embodied by leaders such as Robert F. Kennedy and Martin Luther King Jr., was rendered even more poignant by their assassinations.

At the same time, many gay men and lesbians were beginning to lose patience with a society that spent their tax dollars, encouraged them to obey its laws, and sent them to fight in its wars, yet reviled them as human beings. Some began to resist the restrictions that forced them to lead double lives, just as they were protesting racial injustice, the Vietnam War, and the oppression of women. While the Stonewall riots of June 1969 came to represent a symbolic, defining moment in the history of the movement, the roots of gay liberation had already taken hold in Boston.

The establishment of Boston's Mattachine Society chapter continued a trend that had begun in 1950, when Harry Hay founded its first chapter in Los Angeles. Lesbians in San Francisco and New York founded the Daughters of Bilitis (DOB) on the Mattachine model. In 1965 an article appeared in the *Mid-Town Journal* announcing an appearance by the president of DOB's New York chapter at a hotel in Brookline to discuss the formation of a Boston chapter. The Boston branch was eventually formed in 1969.

The Boston chapter of Mattachine sponsored discussions, lectures, and a newsletter. The group invited speakers from New York or gathered to hear tapes from some of the country's first conferences on the causes and treatment of, and social and legal issues concerning, homosexuality. For many members, these experiences provided their first substantive evidence that homosexuality was a widespread phenomenon that could be discussed as something other than a crime. The chapter was dissolved after several years.

Though the Mattachine and Demophile Societies had gained some visibility through public forums in the late 1950s and early 1960s, most gay Bostonians were unaware of their activities. Frank Morgan describes the night in February 1968 that NBC television aired a white paper entitled "Homosexuality in America."

I was at my brother's house and he said, "Aw, I don't want to watch that baloney." And I said, "Well, I'm going to go home." I ran all the way—almost killed myself trying to get over the snowbanks so I'd be home on time. Lo and behold, there was Dick Leitsch, who was then president of Mattachine New York. That was when I became aware that there were national, even international things going on.

I guess it was like a bridal night. It was like everything was wonderful. I realized that, anyplace you can go, you can find people to like, you can find people to sleep with, you can find people to hang out with. That amazed me, because I always thought that what I felt was something that happened in the dark. And it was, in my lifetime—up until that moment.[27]

The following year, in January 1969, six months before Stonewall, Morgan would hold a meeting at the Arlington Street Church to establish a group that became the Homophile Union of Boston, one of the city's first gay political groups.

Over the next three decades, the climate in Boston would change dramatically. In 1973 *Gay Community News,* the first national lesbian and gay weekly newspaper, would begin publication. The following year, Elaine Noble would be elected as the country's first openly gay state representative. Gerry Studds and Barney Frank would become the country's first openly gay congressmen. In 1989 the Massachusetts legislature would pass a lesbian and gay civil rights bill. Frank Morgan's mad dash through the snow can be seen as part of the larger chain of events that would soon bring lesbians and gay men—in Boston and across the country—to the forefront of the nation's consciousness and its history.

Afterword

The origins of The History Project date back to November 1979, when Allan Bérubé of the San Francisco Lesbian and Gay History Project delivered a lecture entitled "Lesbian Masquerades: Passing Women" at the Old Cambridge Baptist Church. After the lecture, a group of those in attendance decided to begin the process of researching the history of Boston's lesbian and gay communities. The collective that they formed became the Boston Area Lesbian and Gay History Project (BALGHP), which met weekly for the next several years. Members of BALGHP included Marla Allison, Ann Bissett, Liana Borghia, Libby Bouvier, Chris Czernik, Smokey Eule, Pat Gozemba, Steve Harrington, Barbara Henry, Joe Interrante, Beth Kelly, Jan Lambertz, Bob MacHenry, Mark MacKay, Shelley Mains, Linda Moody, Sal Ramaci, Bob Skiba, Abby Solomon, and Chris Waters.

When the City of Boston celebrated its three-hundred-fiftieth anniversary in 1980, BALGHP was awarded a grant of $500 from the city to pursue its historical research. The group wrote an article that was published in conjunction with the Jubilee 350 celebration. They had already begun to develop a slide show entitled "Our Boston Heritage: 350 Years of Lesbian and Gay History," which would be used to present the results of their research to the public. The slide show was eventually presented at dozens of bars, meetings, and conferences across the United States and in Europe. Other projects included gathering oral histories of lesbian and gay bar patrons, writing a series of articles for *Gay Community News,* and researching a timeline of Boston lesbian and gay community groups. Later in the 1980s, a number of factors led to a thinning and dispersal of the group—including AIDS and breast cancer. Several members of BALGHP kept the organization active, however, and continued to present and refine the slide show.

During 1994 many Bostonians attended the *Becoming Visible* exhibit mounted at the New York Public Library in conjunction with the twenty-fifth anniversary of the Stonewall rebellion. Inspired by the exhibit, a group of individuals resolved to create an exhibit on the lesbian and gay history of Boston, using BALGHP's slide show as a point of departure. The group soon coalesced into the organization now known as The History Project.

Research efforts associated with the exhibit revealed once again the need for a permanent archives documenting the history of Boston's lesbian and gay communities. We discovered that the vast majority of the subject matter we sought resided in individual hands, where it was difficult to locate and subject to loss or destruction. Other materials were held by institutions that often either had no awareness of their gay historical significance or had an active interest in suppressing that significance. Researching communities that were accustomed to concealing their history proved to be a daunting task.

Despite these difficulties, a treasure trove of information was unearthed. Due to the volume of material, the group's curators decided to limit the exhibit to a comprehensive pre-Stonewall history and a preview of the period from 1970 to 1996. The resulting effort, **Public Faces, Private Lives: Boston's Lesbian and Gay History, 1600–1969,** debuted at the Boston Public Library to considerable acclaim on 31 May 1996. The exhibit, which contained the majority of the material now presented in *Improper Bostonians,* was the most successful in the library's history. We are honored to have had the opportunity to transform that exhibit into this book.

While **Public Faces, Private Lives** was truly the collective effort of many, much of the work was carried out by a core group within The History Project, who assembled the final materials over a period of three months. The curators for the exhibit were Libby Bouvier, Kim Markert, Stephen Nonack, and Nancy Richard. Neal Kane served as the editor for the project; John Kane was the exhibit's designer. These same individuals expanded and revised the exhibit materials to create *Improper Bostonians.*

Other members of The History Project's board—Art Corriveau, John Gordon, Amy Hoffman, Tom Huth, Laura Pattison, and Donna Penn—made invaluable contributions to the creation of both the exhibit and this book, for which they share authorship. In addition, they and board members Stewart Landers, Alan Schwartz, and Denise Simmons have devoted considerable time and energy to realizing the group's organizational goals and project initiatives. These efforts include establishing a permanent lesbian and gay archives at Northeastern University; collecting the oral histories of elders in our community; conducting research into the lives of lesbians and gay men from Boston's communities of color; and sharing our research and

Afterword

The History Project Board of Directors (standing, left to right): Kim Markert, Libby Bouvier, Stewart Landers, Tom Huth, Amy Hoffman, Denise Simmons, John Kane, Neal Kane, John Gordon; (seated, left to right): Stephen Nonack, Nancy Richard, Art Corriveau, and (not pictured) Alan Schwartz

expertise with other groups and individuals. Work continues on an exhibit documenting our community's history in the post-Stonewall era. We remain a grassroots, all-volunteer organization.

In assembling *Improper Bostonians,* our intent has been to provide an annotated sourcebook that will serve as the basis for additional research and scholarship and provide a fount of insight, inspiration, and delight to gay people and others, both in the Boston area and throughout the country.

The History Project
46 Pleasant Street
Cambridge, Massachusetts
02139

January 1998

Documentary notes

A Puritan heritage: The seventeenth century

1. John Demos, *The Little Commonwealth: Family Life in Plymouth Colony* (New York: Oxford University Press, 1970), 77; Richard P. Gildrie, *The Profane, the Civil & the Godly: The Reformation of Manners in Orthodox New England, 1679–1749* (University Park: Pennsylvania State University Press, 1994), 85; Edmund S. Morgan, *The Puritan Family: Religion and Domestic Relations in Seventeenth-Century New England* (New York: Harper & Row, 1966), 140.

2. Alan Bray, *Homosexuality in Renaissance England* (London: GMP Publishers, 1982), 26; Jonathan Ned Katz, *Gay/Lesbian Almanac: A New Documentary* (New York: Harper & Row, 1983), 41.

3. Richard Godbeer, "'The Cry of Sodom': Discourse, Intercourse, and Desire in Colonial New England," *The William and Mary Quarterly,* 3d ser., vol. 52, no. 2 (April 1995), 281, n.91; Katz, *Almanac,* 108, 118. For a contrasting view of the frequency of sodomy among early Puritans, see Roger Thompson, *Sex in Middlesex: Popular Mores in a Massachusetts County, 1649–1699* (Amherst: University of Massachusetts Press, 1986), 74.

4. Jack Greene, "Colonial New England in Recent Historiography," in *Interpreting Early America,* ed. Jack Greene (Charlottesville: University Press of Virginia, 1996), 253; Thomas H. O'Connor, *Bibles, Brahmins and Bosses: A Short History of Boston* (Boston: Trustees of the Public Library of the City of Boston, 1991), 37-39.

5. Will Roscoe, *Living the Spirit: A Gay American Indian Anthology* (New York: St. Martin's Press, 1988), 217; Walter L. Williams, *The Spirit and the Flesh: Sexual Diversity in American Indian Culture* (Boston: Beacon Press, 1986), 57.

6. Kathleen Bragdon, *Native People of Southern New England: 1500-1650* (Norman: University of Oklahoma Press, 1996), 177, 200.

7. Katz, *Almanac,* 39.

8. Katz, *Almanac,* 74-118.

9. Alan Bray, "Homosexuality and the Signs of Male Friendship in Elizabethan England," in *Queering the Renaissance,* ed. Jonathan Goldberg (Durham, N.C.: Duke University Press, 1994), 56. Rictor Norton, *Mother Clap's Molly House: The Gay Subculture in England, 1700–1830* (London: GMP Publishers, 1992), 21.

10. Michael Warner, "New English Sodom," in *Queering the Renaissance,* ed. Jonathan Goldberg (Durham, N.C.: Duke University Press, 1994), 330-352; John Winthrop, *Winthrop Papers,* vol. 2 (Boston: Massachusetts Historical Society, 1931), 203-206.

11. Jonathan Ned Katz, *Gay American History* (New York: Meridian, 1992), 22.

12. Jonathan Goldberg, *Sodometries: Renaissance Texts, Modern Sexualities* (Stanford, Calif.: Stanford University Press, 1992), 234.

13. Goldberg, 234.

14. Richard Slotkin, *Regeneration through Violence* (Middletown, Conn.: Wesleyan University Press, 1973), 59, 63. See also John Canup, *Out of the Wilderness: The Emergence of an American Identity in Colonial New England* (Middletown, Conn.: Wesleyan University Press, 1990), 29-50.

15. Nicholas Noyes, "An Essay Against Periwigs," in *Remarkable Providences: 1600–1760,* ed. John Demos (New York: George Braziller, 1972), 214-218; Roger Thompson, "Attitudes towards Homosexuality in the Seventeenth-Century New England Colonies," *Journal of American Studies,* vol. 23, no. 1 (1989): 34-40. See also Bruce C. Daniels, *Puritans at Play: Leisure and Recreation in Colonial New England* (New York: St. Martin's Press, 1995), 67; Daniels discusses the Puritan association of theater, cross-dressing, and sodomy.

16. *Essex County Quarterly Court Records and Files,* 341.

17. *New Hampshire Court Records,* 96.

18. Katz, *Almanac,* 55.

19. *Records and Files of the Quarterly Courts of Essex County,* ed. George Francis Dow (Salem, Mass.: The Essex Institute, 1911), vol. 1, 44. The original record is in *The Essex County Quarterly Court Record Book,* vol. 2 (1638–1648), 123.

20. *Records of the Colony of New Plymouth,* ed. Nathaniel B. Shurtleff (Boston: William White, 1855), Court Orders: Vol. II (1641–1651), 163.

21. Alan Bray, *Homosexuality,* 92; Robert Oaks, "'Things Fearful to Name': Sodomy and Buggery in Seventeenth-Century New England," *Journal of Social History,* vol. 12, no. 2 (1978): 272.

22. Katz, *Almanac,* 82-84.

23. Katz, *Almanac,* 94-100; Michael Wigglesworth, *The Diary of Michael Wigglesworth, 1653–1657: The Conscience of a Puritan,* ed. Edmund S. Morgan (Gloucester, Mass.: Peter Smith, 1970).

24. Katz, *Almanac,* 123.

25. Gildrie, 201.

Boston in transition: The eighteenth century

1. Cornelia Hughes Dayton, "Turning Points and the Relevance of Colonial Legal History," *The William and Mary Quarterly,* 3d ser., vol. 50, no. 1 (January 1994): 11-12; Susan Justin, *Disorderly Women: Sexual Politics and Evangelicalism in Revolutionary New England* (Ithaca, N.Y.: Cornell University Press, 1994), 103; Emil Oberholzer, *Delinquent Saints: Disciplinary Actions in the Early Congregational Churches of Massachusetts* (New York: Columbia University Press, 1956), 126-135.

2. Richard Godbeer, "'The Cry of Sodom': Discourse, Intercourse, and Desire in Colonial New England," *The William and Mary Quarterly,* 3d ser., vol. 52, no. 2 (April 1995): 272, 277; Confession of Stephen Gorton, 27 October, 1756, Box 7, Isaac Backus Papers, Trask Memorial Library, Andover Newton Theological School; *Church Records,* Old North Congregational Church, Marblehead, Massachusetts, 72, 74; Christine Heyrman, *Commerce and Culture: The Maritime Communities of Colonial Massachusetts 1690–1750* (New York: W. W. Norton, 1984), 285-286.

3. Nancy F. Cott, *The Bonds of Womanhood: "Women's Sphere" in New England, 1780–1835* (New Haven: Yale University Press, 1977), 161, 170; Carol F. Karlsen and Laurie Crumpacker, Introduction in *The Journal of Esther Edwards Burr: 1754–1757,* ed. Carol F. Karlsen and Laurie Crumpacker (New Haven: Yale University Press, 1984), 183; Carroll Smith-Rosenberg, "The Female World of Love and Ritual: Relations between

Women in Nineteenth-Century America," *Signs: Journal of Women in Culture and Society,* vol. 1, no. 1 (1975): 8.

4. Esther Edwards Burr, *The Journal,* 89, 92, 118, 257, 307.

5. Carl Bridenbaugh, *Cities in the Wilderness,* 277; Alan Sinfield, *The Wilde Century: Effeminacy, Oscar Wilde and the Queer Moment* (New York: Columbia University Press, 1994), 27, 33.

6. Thomas Hutchinson, *Hutchinson's History of Massachusetts Bay,* ed. Laurence Shaw Mayo (Cambridge, Mass.: Harvard University Press, 1936), 114.

7. Pearl Binder, *Muffs and Morals* (New York: Morrow, 1954), 46.

8. "The Conjuror-No. III, A Chapter of Beaux," *Columbian Centinel and Massachusetts Federalist,* vol. 33, no. 15 (Wednesday, 23 April 1800): 1.

9. Jonathan Ned Katz, *Gay American History* (New York: Meridian, 1992), 212-214.

10. Unpublished research of Catherine Kaplan provided to The History Project, 1996.

11. *Anthology Society: Journal of the Proceedings of the Society,* introduction by M. A. DeWolfe Howe (1910): 13; Kaplan; Harold Kirker and James Kin, *Bulfinch's Boston: 1787–1817* (New York: Oxford University Press, 1964), 216.

The Athens of America: The nineteenth century

205

1. Boston Area Lesbian and Gay History Project, slide show script (unpublished).

2. *The Journals and Miscellaneous Notebooks of Ralph Waldo Emerson* (Cambridge, Mass.: Harvard University Press, 1960), vol. 1.

3. *The Collected Works of Ralph Waldo Emerson* (Cambridge, Mass.: Harvard University Press, 1979), vol. 2, 111.

4. Robert D. Richardson Jr., *Henry Thoreau: A Life of the Mind* (Berkeley: University of California Press, 1989).

5. *Richardson,* 58.

6. Hershel Parker, *Herman Melville: A Biography* (Baltimore: Johns Hopkins University Press, 1996), vol. 1, 748.

7. James R. Mellow, *Nathaniel Hawthorne in His Times* (Boston: Houghton Mifflin, 1980), 378-379.

8. Harrison Hayford, *Melville's "Monody": Really for Hawthorne?* (Evanston, Ill.: Northwestern University Press, 1990); *Collected Poems of Herman Melville*, ed. Howard P. Vincent (Chicago: Hendricks House, 1947), 228.

9. Mellow, 348; *Herman Melville, Clarel: A Poem and Pilgrimage in the Holy Land*, ed. Walter E. Bezanson (New York: Hendricks House, 1960), xciv.

10. *Memoirs of Margaret Fuller Ossoli,* ed. Ralph Waldo Emerson (Boston: Brown, Taggard and Chase, 1860), vol. 1; Joan von Mehren, *Minerva and the Muse: A Life of Margaret Fuller* (Amherst: University of Massachusetts Press, 1994).

Documentary notes

11. Rebecca Patterson, *The Riddle of Emily Dickinson* (Boston: Houghton Mifflin, 1951).

12. Donald Yacovone, "'Surpassing the Love of Women': Male Friendships and the Social Construction of Masculinity before Freud" (unpublished essay); Yacovone, "Abolitionists and the Language of Fraternal Love," in *Meanings for Manhood: Constructions of Masculinity in Victorian America* (Chicago: University of Chicago Press, 1990); *Record of Service of the Forty-Fourth Massachusetts Volunteer Militia* (Boston: Privately printed, 1887), 257.

13. Mary Thacher Higginson, *Thomas Wentworth Higginson: The Story of His Life* (Boston: Houghton Mifflin, 1914).

14. Nicolai Cikovsky Jr., *Winslow Homer* (New Haven: Yale University Press, 1995); Albert Warren Kelsey, *Autobiographical Notes and Memoranda* (Baltimore, Md.: Munder-Thomson Press, 1911).

15. Eugene Tompkins, *The History of the Boston Theater, 1854–1901* (reprint, New York: Benjamin Blom, 1969).

16. Lisa Merrill, *When Romeo Was a Woman: Charlotte Cushman and Her Circle of Female Spectators* (Ann Arbor: University of Michigan Press, forthcoming, 1998).

17. Joseph Leach, *Bright Particular Star: The Life and Times of Charlotte Cushman* (New Haven: Yale University Press, 1970), 272.

18. *History of Woman Suffrage,* ed. Elizabeth C. Stanton (New York: Fowler & Wells, 1881), 828.

19. Margaret Farrand Thorp, in *Notable American Women, 1607–1950* (Cambridge, Mass.: Harvard University Press, 1971), vol. 1; William Wetmore Story, *Excursions in Art and Letters* (Boston: Houghton Mifflin, 1891); Dolly Sherwood, *Harriet Hosmer, American Sculptor, 1830–1908* (Columbia: University of Missouri Press, 1991).

20. Lynda Roscoe Hartigan, in *Black Women in America: An Historical Encyclopedia* (Brooklyn: Carlson Publishing, 1993), vol. 1; Timothy Anglin Burgard, "Edmonia Lewis and Henry Wadsworth Longfellow: Images and Identities" (Cambridge, Mass.: Fogg Art Museum, 1995). Historian Marilyn Richardson is currently at work on a biography of Lewis.

21. Boston Area Lesbian and Gay History Project, slide show script (unpublished).

22. Nancy Sahli, "Smashing: Women's Relationships before the Fall," *Chrysalis*, no. 8 (1979).

23. Jean Strouse, *Alice James, a Biography* (Boston: Houghton Mifflin, 1980); R. W. B. Lewis, *The Jameses: A Family Narrative* (New York: Farrar, Straus & Giroux, 1991).

24. Patricia Ann Palmieri, *In Adamless Eden: The Community of Women Faculty at Wellesley* (New Haven: Yale University Press, 1995). Papers of the Wellesley College faculty are preserved in the Wellesley College Archives.

25. Elizabeth Brown-Guillory, in *Black Women in America* (Brooklyn: Carlson Publishing, 1993) vol. 1; Gloria T. Hull, "The Buried Life and Poetry of Angelina Weld Grimké," *Conditions*, vol. 2, no. 2 (Autumn 1979).

26. Theresa Corcoran, in *Notable American Women: The Modern Period* (Cambridge, Mass.: Harvard University Press, 1980).

27. Edith Guerrier, *An Independent Woman: The Autobiography of Edith Guerrier*, ed. Molly Matson (Amherst: University of Massachusetts Press, 1992).

28. Kate Clifford Larson, "The Saturday Evening Girls: A Social Experiment in Class Bridging and Cross Cultural Female Dominion Building in Turn of the Century Boston," thesis (Simmons College, 1995).

29. *Memoir of Susan Dimock: Resident Physician of the New England Hospital for Women and Children* (Boston: Press of J. Wilson, 1875).

30. Mercedes M. Randall, *Improper Bostonian: Emily Greene Balch* (New York: Twayne, 1964). The papers of Emily Greene Balch are held at the Swarthmore College Peace Collection.

31. Estelle Jussim, *Slave to Beauty: The Eccentric Life and Controversial Career of F. Holland Day, Photographer, Publisher, Aesthete* (Boston: David R. Godine, 1981).

32. James F. Crump, *F. Holland Day: Suffering the Ideal* (Santa Fe, N.M.: Twin Palms, 1995).

33. Codman Papers, Society for the Preservation of New England Antiquities.

34. Jussim.

35. Douglass Shand-Tucci, *Ralph Adams Cram: Life and Architecture* (Amherst: University of Massachusetts Press, 1994), vol. 1.

36. Trevor J. Fairbrother, "A Private Album: John Singer Sargent's Drawings of Nude Male Models," *Arts*, vol. 56, December 1981.

37. *Beauport Chronicle: The Intimate Letters of Henry Davis Sleeper to Abram Piatt Andrew Jr. 1906–1915* (Boston: Society for the Preservation of New England Antiquities, 1991); Douglass Shand-Tucci, *The Art of Scandal: The Life and Times of Isabella Stewart Gardner* (New York: HarperCollins, 1997).

38. Louise Hall Tharp, *Mrs. Jack: A Biography of Isabella Stewart Gardner* (Boston: Little, Brown, 1965); Thornton Oakley, *Cecilia Beaux* (Philadelphia: H. Biddle Printing Co., 1943).

39. Martin Green, *The Mount Vernon Street Warrens: A Boston Story, 1860–1910* (New York: Charles Scribner's Sons, 1989); David Sox, *Bachelors of Art: Edward Perry Warren and the Lewes House Brotherhood* (London: Fourth Estate, 1991).

40. Catherine L. Seiberling, *A Study Report of the Gibson House Museum: 137 Beacon Street, Boston, Massachusetts* (Boston: Gibson House, 1991).

41. Shand-Tucci, *The Art of Scandal*.

The early twentieth century: 1900–1945

1. John D'Emilio, "Capitalism and Gay Identity," in *Powers of Desire: The Politics of Sexuality,* ed. Ann Snitow, Christine Stansell, and Sharon Thompson (New York: Monthly Review Press, 1983), 100–113; Boston Area Lesbian and Gay History Project, "Our Boston Heritage" slide show script (unpublished).

208

2. Allan Bérubé, *Coming Out under Fire: The History of Gay Men and Women in World War Two* (New York: Free Press, 1990); George Chauncey, *Gay New York: Gender, Urban Culture, and the Making of the Gay Male World, 1890–1940* (New York: Basic Books, 1994); Jonathan Ned Katz, *Gay American History: Lesbians and Gay Men in the U.S.A.: A Documentary History* (New York: Meridian, 1992).

3. Kirstin Gay Esterberg, "From Illness to Action: Conceptions of Homosexuality in *The Ladder,* 1956-1965," *Journal of Sex Research,* vol. 27, no. 1 (1990): 65-80; Jonathan Ned Katz, *Gay/Lesbian Almanac: A New Documentary* (New York: Harper & Row, 1983); Katz, *Gay American History;* Boston Area Lesbian and Gay History Project, slide show script.

4. Katz, *Gay American History,* 382-383.

5. Katz, *Almanac,* 294.

6. F. O. Matthiessen, *The Rat and the Devil: Journal Letters of F. O. Matthiessen and Russell Cheney,* ed. Louis Hyde (Boston: Alyson Publications, 1988).

7. Joanna Davenport, in *Notable American Women: The Modern Period* (Cambridge, Mass.: Harvard University Press, 1980).

8. Marjorie Garber, *Vested Interests: Cross-Dressing and Cultural Anxiety* (New York: Routledge, 1992); Sharon R. Ullman, "'The Twentieth Century Way': Female Impersonation and Sexual Practice in Turn-of-the-Century America," *Journal of the History of Sexuality,* vol. 5, no. 4 (1995): 573-601.

9. Eugene Tompkins, *The History of the Boston Theatre, 1854–1901* (Reprint, New York: Benjamin Blom, 1969).

10. Karl Schrifftgiesser, "How Little Rollo Came to Rule the Mind of Boston: History of the Censorship of Plays and Books That Attracts the Attention of the Country," in *The Boston Transcript,* 21 September 1929, magazine section; William Robert Reardon, "Banned in Boston: A Study of Theatrical Censorship in Boston from 1630 to 1950" (Ph.D. diss., Stanford University, 1952).

11. Records of the Boston Office of the Clerk of Committees. Proceedings of 1892 meeting, Boston Archives and Record Management Division.

12. Papers of the New England Watch and Ward Society. Harvard Law School Library, Manuscripts Unit.

13. Boston Area Lesbian and Gay History Project, slide show script.

14. Papers of the New England Watch and Ward Society.

15. Robert G. interviewed by Nancy Richard, audio cassette, 25 September 1995, The History Project collection.

16. Richard Cowen papers, Boston Athenæum.

17. Boston Area Lesbian and Gay History Project, slide show script.

18. Conrad S. interviewed by Nancy Richard, audio cassette, 22 July 1995, The History Project collection.

19. Jean S. interviewed by Nancy Richard, audio cassette, 9 November 1997, The History Project collection.

20. Louise Y. interviewed by Nancy Richard, audio cassette, 9 November 1997, The History Project collection.

21. Anthony Tommasini, *Virgil Thomson: Composer on the Aisle* (New York: W. W. Norton, 1997); Katz, *Gay American History,* 584-585.

22. Gore Vidal interviewed by John Mitzel for *Fag Rag,* 1974. Transcript in The History Project collection.

23. Anonymous, *The Limerick,* ed. Gershon Legman, submitted to The History Project by Robbie Lohnes, Cambridge, Massachusetts.

24. Preston C. interviewed by Nancy Richard, audio cassette, 21 April 1997, The History Project collection.

From the Cold War to Stonewall: 1945–1969

1. Allan Bérubé and John D'Emilio, "The Military and Lesbians during the McCarthy Years," *Signs: Journal of Women in Culture and Society,* vol. 9, no. 4 (Summer 1984): 759-775.

2. Senate Subcommittee on Expenditures in the Executive Department, Subcommittee on Investigations, *Employment of Homosexuals and Other Sex Perverts in Government,* 81st Cong., 2d sess., 1950, S. Doc. 241, serial 11401.

3. Louise Y. interviewed by Nancy Richard, audio cassette, 9 November 1997, The History Project collection.

4. Estelle B. Freedman, *Maternal Justice: Miriam Van Waters and the Female Reform Tradition* (Chicago: University of Chicago Press, 1996).

5. "Remarks Made by Anne L. Clark, M.D., at Hodder Hall Massachusetts Correctional Institution for Women, Framingham, Massachusetts" (unpublished), 13 May 1959.

6. Iben Snupin, *Reeling Around* (Boston: Journal Publishing, 1945).

7. Richard Shibley, in a telephone conversation with editor's son, 1996.

8. Bob R. interviewed by Nancy Richard, audio cassette, 12 October 1997. The History Project collection.

9. Papers of the New England Watch and Ward Society.

10. Alice F. interviewed by Nancy Richard, audio cassette, 6 December 1995. The History Project collection.

11. Joy B. interviewed by Nancy Richard, audio cassette, 21 September 1997. The History Project collection.

12. Stephen A. Twinward, history of the Boston bars in *Esplanade,* 1976-1978. Information in this series was used throughout this section.

13. Mr. G. interviewed by Nancy Richard, audio cassette, 9 December 1995. The History Project collection.

14. Barbara H. interviewed by Nancy Richard, audio cassette, 21 August 1997. The History Project collection.

15. Helaine Z. interviewed by Nancy Richard, audio cassette, 28 December 1995. The History Project collection.

16. Stephen A. Twinward, *Esplanade.*

210

17. Chester S. interview with Nancy Richard, audio cassette, 18 October 1997. The History Project collection.

18. G. F. Caswell, *Boston: Today* (Boston: Beacon Hill Press, 1952).

19. Sylvia Sidney interviewed by Nancy Richard, audio cassette, 13 April 1996. The History Project collection.

20. Francis Toohey, "The First Beaux Arts Ball," *Esplanade,* October 1976.

21. Paul M. interviewed by Nancy Richard, audio cassette and video tape, 7 September 1997. The History Project collection.

22. Thomas H. O'Connor, *Building a New Boston: Politics and Urban Renewal, 1950–1970* (Boston: Northeastern University Press, 1993).

23. Records of the Boston City Council. Proceedings of the Committee on Urban Renewal, 7 July 1965. Boston Archives and Record Management Division.

24. Letter to Ralph Gillis, founding member of Boston chapter of the Mattachine Society, from member of the New York Mattachine Society, 14 January 1957, unsigned. International Gay Information Center Archives, Rare Books and Manuscripts Division, New York Public Library.

25. Letter to member of New York Mattachine from member of Boston Mattachine Society, 29 October 1957, unsigned. International Gay Information Center Archives, Rare Books and Manuscripts Division, New York Public Library.

26. Letter to Prescott Townsend from Curtis Dewees, officer of the New York Mattachine Society, 7 December 1959. International Gay Information Center Archives, Rare Books and Manuscripts Division, New York Public Library. Boston writer Adrian Cathcart is completing a biography of Prescott Townsend. Townsend is captured on film in Andy Meyer's "An Early Clue to the New Direction" (1966).

27. Frank Morgan interviewed by Nancy Richard, audio cassette, 26 November 1995. The History Project collection.

Picture credits

xii John Kane.

5 Massachusetts Historical Society, Boston.

8-9 Unpublished thesis, Boston Architectural Center, 1994.

10 Facsimile from *Massachusetts Historical Collections,* vol. Third series, VIII, 1935.

13 Boston Athenæum, Boston, Print Room.

14 Above: Published in *Story of America in Pictures,* Arranged by Alan C. Collins (New York: Doubleday Doran & Co., 1935). Below: The History Project collection.

15 Massachusetts Historical Society.

16 Top: Massachusetts Archives. Massachusetts Archives collection, Boston. Bottom: Judicial Archives, Massachusetts Archives, Boston.

19 Judicial Archives.

20 The History Project collection.

21 Both: Boston Athenæum.

22 Boston Athenæum.

23 American Antiquarian Society, Worcester, Mass.

24 Trask Memorial Library, Andover Newton Theological School, Newton, Mass.

27 Yale University Art Gallery, Bequest of Oliver Burr Jennings, B.A. 1917, in memory of Miss Annie Burr Jennings.

28 Boston Athenæum, Print Room.

29 Above: Peabody Essex Museum, Salem, Mass. Below: Boston Public Library, Microtext Department.

30 Left: *The Female Review: Life of Deborah Sampson, the Female Soldier in the War of Revolution* (Dedham, 1797), Boston Athenæum, Print Room. Right: Judicial Archives.

32 Boston Athenæum, Print Room.

33 Left: Judicial Archives. Right: Massachusetts Historical Society.

34 Boston Athenæum, Print Room.

35 Massachusetts Historical Society.

36 Boston Athenæum, Print Room.

37 Right: Portrait, Boston Athenæum, Print Room. Left: Boston Athenæum.

41 Trustees of the Boston Public Library, Research Division.

43 Above: Boston Athenæum, Print Room. Below: Published in *Journals and Miscellaneous Notebooks of R.W. Emerson,* vol. 1.

44 Boston Athenæum, Print Room.

45 Boston Athenæum, Print Room.

46 Boston Athenæum, Print Room.

48 Both: Boston Athenæum, Print Room.

49 Postcard published by Amherst College in The History Project collection.

50 Above: Boston Athenæum. Below: Boston Athenæum, Print Room.

51 Both: Massachusetts Historical Society.

52 Massachusetts Historical Society.

53 Boston Athenæum, Print Room.

54 Massachusetts Historical Society.

55 Published in *The Outlook,* vol. 59, 2 July 1898.

56 The History Project collection.

57 Boston Athenæum, Print Room.

58 Left: Schlesinger Library, Radcliffe College, carte de visite by Wendroth & Taylor. Right: Boston Athenæum, Susan Freeman Lawrence, *Family history and reminiscences,* 1897 (ms.).

59 Above left: The Harvard Theater Collection, The Houghton Library. Below left: Boston Athenæum, Print Room. Right: Schlesinger Library, Radcliffe College, carte de visite by Sonrel, Boston.

60 Right: Schlesinger Library, Radcliffe College, carte de visite by Marianecci. Left: Boston Athenæum.

61 Schlesinger Library, Radcliffe College.

62 The History Project collection.

63 Boston Athenæum, Print Room.

64 Boston Athenæum, Print Room.

65 Both: Boston Athenæum, Elizabeth Brewster Ely Papers.

67 The College Archives, Simmons College, Boston.

68 Boston Athenæum, Print Room.

70 Above: Wellesley College Archives, Wellesley, Mass., photo by Knackstedt & Nather, 1890. Below: Wellesley College Archives.

71 Houghton Library, Harvard University, Cambridge.

72 Both: Boston Athenæum, Print Room.

73 Above left: Wellesley College Archives, photo by Longfellow Gallery, Portland, Maine. Below left: Wellesley College Archives, from Class of 1900 Class Book, photo by Notman. Right: Wellesley College Archives.

74 Wellesley College Archives.

75 Boston Athenæum, Print Room.

76 Yale Collection of American Literature, Beinecke Rare Book and Manuscript Library.

77 Left: Moorland-Spingard Research Center, Howard University, Washington, D.C. Right: Wellesley College Archives, photo by Henry Bowen Brainerd.

78 Old Dartmouth Historical Society, New Bedford Whaling Museum, New Bedford, Mass.

79 Both: Old Dartmouth Historical Society, New Bedford Whaling Museum.

80 Old Dartmouth Historical Society, New Bedford Whaling Museum.

81 The College Archives, Simmons College.

82 *Memoir of Susan Dimock: Resident Physician of the New England Hospital for Women and Children* (Boston, 1875).

83 Both: Schlesinger Library, Radcliffe College.

84 Above: Boston Athenæum, Print Room. Below: Boston Athenæum.

85 Both: Norwood Historical Society, Norwood, Mass.

86 Top: Society for the Preservation of New England Antiquities, Codman Papers. Middle above: Boston Athenæum. Middle below: Society for the Preservation of New England Antiquities, Codman Papers. Bottom: Boston Athenæum.

87 College of the Holy Cross, Worcester, Mass.

88 Above: Published in *Camera Notes,* vol. II, no. 1, July 1898. Below: Published in *Kahlil Gibran: His Life and World* (Boston: New York Graphic Society, 1974) by Jean Gibran and Kahlil Gibran. Courtesy of Jean Gibran and Kahlil Gibran.

89 Far left: Boston Athenæum. Left: Boston Athenæum, Print Room. Right: Society for the Preservation of New England Antiquities, Codman Papers. Far right: Boston Athenæum, published in Harvard College, *Class of 1895, 25th Anniversary Report* (Cambridge: University Press, 1920).

90 Both: A. Piatt Andrew Archive, Society for the Preservation of New England Antiquities, courtesy of Andrew Gray.

91 Right: A. Piatt Andrew Archive.
Left: Fogg Art Museum, Harvard University Art Museum, Gift of Mrs. Francis Ormond.

92 A. Piatt Andrew Archive.

93 Left: Gift of E. P. Warren, Courtesy of Museum of Fine Arts, Boston.
Right: Published in Osbert Burdett, *Edward Perry Warren: The Biography of a Connoisseur* (London: Christophers, 1941).

94 Above: Published in *Life* magazine, 24 March 1941, courtesy of Gibson House Museum, Boston.
Below: Boston Athenæum.

95 Top: Published in *The Silver Wedding of the Bear: A Memorial of the Celebration of the Twenty-Fifth Anniversary of the Tavern Club, 15 January 1909* (Boston: Club of Odd Volumes, 1910).
Bottom: Published in *Harvard Hasty Pudding Club, The Dynamiters: A Burlesque in Three Acts* (Cambridge: University Press, 1901).

96 Collection of Deb Edel.

100 The History Project collection.

103 Yale Collection of American Literature, Beinecke Rare Book and Manuscript Library.

104 The History Project collection.

105 The History Project collection.

107 All: The History Project collection.

108 The History Project collection.

109 Associated Press photo, Boston Athenæum, Print Room.

110 Boston Athenæum, Broadside Collection.

111 Boston Athenæum, Theater Collection.

113 Harvard Theater Collection, Houghton Library.

114 Boston Public Library, Print Department, *Herald-Traveler* collection.

115 Boston Public Library, Print Department, *Herald-Traveler* collection.

117 Northeastern University Libraries Archives and Special Collections Department.

118 The College Archives, Simmons College.

119 Both: The College Archives, Simmons College.

120 Left: Massachusetts Archives.
Right: The History Project collection.

122 Top: Boston Public Library, Print Department, *Herald-Traveler* collection.
Left: The History Project collection.
Right: The History Project collection.

125 Boston Athenæum, Stewart Mitchell papers.

126 Boston Athenæum, David M. K. McKibbin papers.

128 Both: The History Project collection.

129 The History Project collection.

130 *Boston Globe.*

131 Boston Public Library, Print Department, photograph by Leslie Jones.

133 Collection of Jean S.

134 Collection of Jean S.

135 Above: Collection of Jean S.
Below: Collection of Louise Y.

136 Boston Public Library, Print Department, *Herald-Traveler* collection.

139 Both: The History Project collection (donated by Preston Claridge).

140 The History Project collection (donated by Preston Claridge).

141 Both: The History Project collection (donated by Preston Claridge).

142 The History Project collection.

143 Both: The College Archives, Simmons College. Maida Herman Solomon papers.

145 The History Project collection.

146 All: Boston Public Library, Print Department, *Herald-Traveler* collection.

155 Iben Snupin, *Reeling Around* (Boston, 1945), The History Project collection (donated by Richard Shibley).

156 Collection of Louise Y.

157 Left: Boston Public Library, Microtext Department.
Right: Collection of Alice Foley.

159 The History Project collection.

160 The History Project collection.

163 Both: Collection of Jim McGrath.

164 Boston Athenæum, Print Room.

165 The History Project collection.

166 Collection of Jim McGrath.

167 Left: Boston Public Library, Print Department, *Herald-Traveler* collection.
Right: Boston Athenæum, George Cushing Collection, Print Room.
Below: Collection of Jim McGrath.

168 Both: The History Project collection.

169 Top: Boston Athenæum, George Cushing Collection, Print Room.
Bottom: *Boston Globe.*

171 Left: Society for the Preservation of New England Antiquities, William T. Clark photograph.
Right: Collection of Bill Conrad.

172 Top: *Boston Globe.*
Bottom: Collection of Jim McGrath.

173 The Bostonian Society/Old State House, Boston.

174 Top: The History Project collection (donated by Jimmy Boynton).
Bottom: The History Project collection.

176 Both: Collection of Robert Reed.

177 Collection of Joy B.

179 The History Project collection.

180 The History Project collection.

181 Collection of Jim McGrath.

182 Both: Collection of Sylvia Sidney.

183 Both: Collection of Sylvia Sidney.

184 The History Project collection.

185 The History Project collection.

187 Collection of Robert Reed.

188 Collection of Robert Reed.

189 Collection of Louise Y.

191 Top: Society for the Preservation of New England Antiquities.
Bottom: *Boston Globe.*

192 Society for the Preservation of New England Antiquities.

194 Private collection of Adrian Cathcart.

196 Both: International Gay Information Center Archives manuscripts and Archives Division, The New York Public Library Astor, Lenox and Tilden Foundation.

197 Collection of Adrian Cathcart.

202 Marilyn Humphries.